Unlocking Global Opportunities: A Guide to Second Passports for Dual Citizenship

ROBERTO MIGUEL RODRIGUEZ

2023

Copyright Page

TITLE: Unlocking Global Opportunities: A Guide to Second Passports for Dual Citizenship

1ST Edition

Copyright @ 2023

ISBN: 9798223760320

Table of Contents

Unlocking Global Opportunities: A Guide to Second Passports for Dual Citizenship

By Roberto Miguel Rodriguez

Introduction:

The index of "Unlocking Global Opportunities: A Guide to Second Passports for Dual Citizenship" serves as a roadmap to navigate through the vast array of information contained within the book. It provides an organized list of topics, allowing readers to quickly locate the specific content they need. Whether you are interested in second passports for dual citizenship, passports for investment, diplomatic passports, high-security passports, or any other niche discussed in this book, the index will guide you to the relevant chapters and subchapters.

Subchapters:

1. Understanding the Concept of Dual Citizenship

- Benefits of dual citizenship

- Factors to consider before acquiring a second passport

2. Second Passport for Dual Citizenship

- Different countries offering second passport programs

- Comparison of eligibility criteria, benefits, and costs

- How to choose the right program for your needs

3. Passports for Investment (Citizenship by Investment)

- Overview of citizenship by investment programs

8. Passports for Medical Tourism (Traveling Abroad for Medical Treatment)

- Advantages of medical tourism passports

- Countries providing medical tourism programs

- Requirements and procedures for obtaining medical tourism passports

9. Student Passports for International Students Studying Abroad

- Benefits of student passports

- Countries with favorable policies for international students

- How to apply for a student passport

10. Passports for Digital Nomads or Remote Workers Looking for Alternative Residency Options

- Overview of digital nomad passports

- Countries offering special residency programs for digital nomads

- Application procedures and requirements

11. Passports for Retirees Seeking Retirement Havens or Pensioner Visas

- Retirement visa programs and benefits

- Countries popular among retirees

- How to obtain a retirement passport or pensioner visa

Conclusion:

The index "Unlocking Global Opportunities: A Guide to Second Passports for Dual Citizenship" provides a comprehensive guide to the various aspects of acquiring a second passport. Whether you are interested in dual citizenship, investment-based passports, diplomatic passports, or any other niche, this index will direct you to the relevant information. By using the index as a reference tool, readers can easily navigate through the book, gaining valuable insights on how to unlock global opportunities and find the ideal passport solution for their unique circumstances.

Chapter 1: Introduction to Second Passports

Understanding the Significance of Second Passports

In today's interconnected world, the concept of citizenship has evolved beyond boundaries and borders. As globalization continues to reshape our lives, individuals are seeking new opportunities that transcend their home country's limitations. This subchapter will delve into the significance of second passports, exploring their various applications and benefits for a diverse range of individuals.

For those seeking dual citizenship, second passports offer immense advantages. Dual citizens enjoy the privileges, rights, and protections of two countries, such as access to healthcare, education, and employment opportunities. Dual citizenship can also provide a safety net during times of political instability, allowing individuals to seek refuge in their secondary country if needed.

Investors looking to expand their global prospects can utilize second passports for citizenship through investment programs. These programs allow individuals to acquire citizenship by making a significant financial contribution to a country. In return, investors gain access to a new market, favorable tax regimes, and enhanced business opportunities. The subchapter will provide insights into the most popular citizenship-by-investment programs worldwide.

Government officials and diplomats can benefit from diplomatic passports, which grant them special privileges and immunities while representing their countries abroad. These passports facilitate travel and diplomatic negotiations, ensuring smooth relations between nations. Understanding the processes and requirements for obtaining diplomatic passports will be crucial for individuals in this niche.

Individuals with high-risk occupations often face security threats and travel restrictions. High-security passports offer advanced features such as biometric data and encryption, ensuring the utmost protection for these individuals. The subchapter will provide a comprehensive overview of the available options and their relevance for individuals in high-risk professions.

Refugees and asylum seekers who are forced to leave their home countries due to conflict or persecution can find solace in second passports. These documents provide them with a legal identity and protection, enabling them to start anew in a different country. The subchapter will explore the avenues available for refugees and asylum seekers to obtain second passports and rebuild their lives.

Business travelers or short-term expatriates often require temporary passports to facilitate their frequent international travels. These passports offer flexibility and convenience, ensuring smooth entry and exit from various countries. The subchapter will highlight the importance of temporary passports for individuals in this niche and provide relevant information on their acquisition.

Moreover, the subchapter will examine the significance of second passports in facilitating medical tourism. Patients traveling abroad for medical treatment can benefit from specialized passports that expedite their access to healthcare services. The subchapter will explore the countries offering such passports and the advantages they provide in the realm of medical tourism.

International students studying abroad can also benefit from dedicated student passports. These passports simplify the visa process and offer additional benefits such as access to student discounts and services. The subchapter will provide insights into the advantages of student passports and the countries that offer them.

For digital nomads or remote workers seeking alternative residency options, second passports provide the freedom to live and work anywhere in the world. The subchapter will delve into the various countries that offer passports suitable for digital nomads, facilitating their nomadic lifestyle.

Lastly, retirees seeking retirement havens or pensioner visas can find second passports invaluable. These passports grant retirees access to pensioner programs, favorable tax regimes, and a higher quality of life. The subchapter will explore the countries that offer retirement havens and the benefits associated with their passport programs.

Understanding the significance of second passports is essential for individuals seeking to unlock global opportunities and transcend the limitations of their home country. This subchapter will serve as a comprehensive guide, providing valuable insights into various passport options and their relevance for individuals in different niches.

Benefits of Dual Citizenship

Dual citizenship refers to the status of an individual who is a citizen of two countries. It offers numerous advantages and opportunities for individuals in various circumstances. This subchapter explores the benefits of dual citizenship for different niches, ranging from investors and government officials to refugees and retirees.

For investors seeking second passports for dual citizenship or citizenship by investment, having dual citizenship can provide greater global mobility and access to international markets. It allows them to expand their business operations, invest in real estate, and diversify their assets in multiple countries. Dual citizens also enjoy the benefits of favorable tax regimes and investment opportunities available in both countries.

Government officials and diplomats with diplomatic passports benefit from dual citizenship by enhancing their ability to represent their home country abroad. It provides them with additional diplomatic privileges and immunities, facilitating their work in international negotiations and diplomatic missions.

Individuals with high-risk occupations, such as journalists, aid workers, or professionals in conflict-prone regions, can greatly benefit from possessing a high-security passport through dual citizenship. This provides them with increased protection and access to consular assistance in times of crisis or emergencies.

For refugees and asylum seekers, acquiring dual citizenship can offer a lifeline and a chance to rebuild their lives in a safe and stable environment. It provides them with legal rights, including access to education, healthcare, and employment opportunities, thus enabling them to integrate into their host country more effectively.

Business travelers or short-term expatriates can benefit from temporary passports obtained through dual citizenship. This allows them to streamline travel procedures, bypass visa restrictions, and expedite entry to various countries, saving time and effort.

Dual citizenship also presents advantages for individuals seeking medical tourism or international students studying abroad. It provides them with the flexibility to travel, study, and receive medical treatment in their home country or the country of their second citizenship, ensuring access to high-quality healthcare and education.

Digital nomads and remote workers looking for alternative residency options can benefit from the flexibility and freedom that dual citizenship offers. It allows them to live and work in different countries, taking advantage of favorable tax regimes, lifestyle choices, and greater opportunities for professional growth.

Lastly, retirees seeking retirement havens or pensioner visas can find dual citizenship as a means to secure their retirement plans. It offers access to countries with attractive retirement benefits, healthcare services, and a high quality of life, ensuring a comfortable and fulfilling retirement experience.

In conclusion, dual citizenship provides a wealth of benefits for individuals across various niches. It offers enhanced global mobility, economic opportunities, legal rights, and protection, making it a valuable asset in today's interconnected world. Whether it is for investment, career advancement, or personal well-being, dual citizenship unlocks a range of global opportunities for individuals seeking to expand their horizons.

Exploring the Different Types of Second Passports

In today's globalized world, the concept of dual citizenship has gained significant popularity among individuals seeking to unlock global opportunities. Owning a second passport can offer a wide range of advantages, including enhanced travel freedom, increased business prospects, and access to better education and healthcare systems. This subchapter aims to delve into the various types of second passports available, catering to the diverse needs of different individuals.

For those interested in dual citizenship, there are several pathways to explore. One of the most common options is obtaining a passport through citizenship by investment programs. These programs allow individuals to make a significant financial investment in a country in exchange for citizenship and a second passport. This option is particularly appealing to entrepreneurs, investors, and high-net-worth individuals looking for international business prospects.

Government officials and diplomats may benefit from diplomatic passports, granting them special privileges and immunities while representing their country abroad. These passports facilitate diplomatic missions and provide access to exclusive diplomatic channels.

Individuals with high-risk occupations, such as journalists, aid workers, or those working in conflict zones, may opt for high-security passports. These passports come with advanced security features and protocols to ensure the safety and protection of individuals in vulnerable situations.

Refugees and asylum seekers often face significant challenges when seeking international protection. However, certain countries offer special refugee passports or travel documents to provide temporary legal status and protection to those in need.

Business travelers or short-term expatriates may benefit from temporary passports, which allow for hassle-free travel during their stay abroad. These passports are particularly useful for individuals who frequently travel for business or work assignments.

Medical tourism has become a popular option for individuals seeking affordable and high-quality medical treatment abroad. Some countries offer special medical tourism passports, facilitating seamless travel and access to specialized healthcare services.

International students studying abroad can obtain student passports, which come with specific benefits such as reduced fees, access to student discounts, and simplified visa processes.

Digital nomads or remote workers looking for alternative residency options can explore passports specifically designed for their needs. These passports cater to individuals who work remotely and prefer a flexible lifestyle with the freedom to live and work from anywhere in the world.

Retirees seeking retirement havens or pensioner visas can benefit from passports that offer attractive retirement programs, including tax incentives, healthcare benefits, and a comfortable lifestyle in retirement-friendly destinations.

In conclusion, the world of second passports offers a plethora of options to individuals seeking dual citizenship. Whether for investment, diplomatic purposes, high-risk occupations, refugee status, temporary stays, medical tourism, education, remote work, or retirement, there is a second passport tailored to meet the unique needs of each individual. By exploring the different types of second passports available, individuals can unlock a world of global opportunities and enjoy the advantages that come with dual citizenship.

Chapter 2: Second Passports for Dual Citizenship

The Concept of Dual Citizenship

Dual citizenship, also known as multiple citizenship, is an intriguing concept that allows individuals to hold the citizenship of two countries simultaneously. This subchapter aims to shed light on the importance and benefits of dual citizenship, catering to a wide range of audiences, including those interested in second passports for dual citizenship, passports for investment, high-security passports, diplomatic passports, and more.

For individuals seeking second passports for dual citizenship, this concept opens up a world of opportunities. It provides the freedom to live, work, study, and travel in two countries without the limitations and restrictions faced by individuals holding a single citizenship. Dual citizenship allows individuals to benefit from the rights, privileges, and protections offered by both countries, such as access to healthcare, education, social welfare, and political participation.

In recent years, the concept of citizenship by investment has gained popularity among those who wish to acquire a second passport through investment. Several countries offer citizenship or residency programs that grant individuals and their families the opportunity to obtain a second passport by making a significant financial contribution to the host country's economy. This avenue has become increasingly attractive to high-net-worth individuals looking to expand their global footprint and enhance their travel and business opportunities.

Government officials and diplomats often require diplomatic passports to facilitate their work on an international stage. These passports provide diplomats with diplomatic immunity and special privileges, enabling them to carry out their duties effectively while representing their home country abroad.

Individuals engaged in high-risk occupations, such as journalists, aid workers, or human rights activists, may require high-security passports that offer enhanced protection and security features. These passports help minimize potential risks and ensure the safety of individuals working in volatile or dangerous environments.

For refugees and asylum seekers, dual citizenship can be a lifeline. It offers them an opportunity to escape persecution, gain legal status, and access basic rights and protections in their host country. Dual citizenship provides a sense of belonging and security to those who have been displaced from their home countries.

Temporary passports cater to business travelers or short-term expatriates who require a travel document for a limited duration. These passports allow individuals to carry out their professional obligations abroad without the hassle of obtaining full citizenship or residency.

Students studying abroad often require student passports to facilitate their educational pursuits. These passports provide international students with the necessary documentation to study, travel, and access various student benefits in their host countries.

Digital nomads and remote workers seeking alternative residency options can benefit from passports that offer flexibility and mobility. These passports allow individuals to live and work in different countries while maintaining their citizenship and enjoying the perks of being a global citizen.

Retirees seeking retirement havens or pensioner visas can explore the option of dual citizenship to secure their future. Certain countries offer retirement programs that provide retirees with long-term residency or citizenship, ensuring a comfortable and fulfilling retirement.

In conclusion, the concept of dual citizenship is a powerful tool that opens up a world of opportunities and benefits for individuals in various niches. Whether it's for investment, diplomatic purposes, high-security needs, or personal circumstances, dual citizenship offers individuals the freedom, flexibility, and security to navigate the complexities of our increasingly interconnected world.

How to Obtain a Second Passport

In today's globalized world, the concept of dual citizenship has become increasingly popular. Many individuals seek the advantages of holding a second passport, whether it be for travel convenience, business opportunities, or personal security. In this subchapter, we will explore the various paths to obtaining a second passport and the different options available to individuals from different backgrounds and interests.

For those looking to obtain a second passport for dual citizenship, there are several routes to consider. Some countries offer citizenship by descent, allowing individuals with a parent or grandparent from that country to apply for citizenship. This can be a relatively straightforward process, requiring the submission of documentation to prove the familial connection.

Another option is citizenship by investment, which is particularly appealing to entrepreneurs and investors. Several countries offer citizenship or residency in exchange for a significant financial contribution, typically through real estate investment or economic development projects. This avenue provides individuals with the opportunity to expand their business horizons while enjoying the benefits of a second passport.

Government officials and diplomats often require diplomatic passports to carry out their duties effectively. In this subchapter, we will explore the specific requirements and procedures involved in obtaining a diplomatic passport. This information will be invaluable for those interested in pursuing a diplomatic career or working in international relations.

Individuals with high-risk occupations, such as journalists or aid workers, may face unique challenges when it comes to travel. High-security passports provide an added layer of protection and can facilitate smoother entry into countries with potential risks. This subchapter will delve into the requirements and benefits of high-security passports for those in high-risk occupations.

Refugees and asylum seekers seeking a new start and a sense of security can also benefit from obtaining a second passport. We will explore the options available to these individuals and guide them through the application process, ensuring they have the necessary information to navigate their new journey.

Business travelers and short-term expatriates often require temporary passports to facilitate their travel. This subchapter will provide guidance on the application process and requirements for obtaining a temporary passport, allowing individuals to travel hassle-free for business purposes.

For those seeking medical treatment abroad, medical tourism passports can streamline the travel and treatment process. This chapter will outline the steps involved in obtaining a medical tourism passport, ensuring individuals can access quality healthcare while enjoying the benefits of a second passport.

International students studying abroad may also desire a second passport to enhance their educational experience and future opportunities. We will address the requirements and benefits of student passports, providing valuable information for those pursuing their academic ambitions overseas.

Digital nomads and remote workers looking for alternative residency options can benefit from second passports that cater to their unique lifestyles. This subchapter will explore the possibilities available to these individuals, ensuring they have the freedom to work and live in different countries.

Lastly, retirees seeking retirement havens or pensioner visas can find valuable information on obtaining a second passport in this subchapter. We will guide them through the process, highlighting countries that offer attractive retirement programs and outlining the requirements for obtaining a retirement-focused passport.

In conclusion, this subchapter provides a comprehensive guide to obtaining a second passport, catering to a diverse range of interests and needs. Whether you are a business person, a government official, a student, or a retiree, the information presented here will help unlock the global opportunities that come with dual citizenship.

Countries Offering Second Passports

In today's globalized world, the concept of dual citizenship has gained considerable popularity, offering individuals a range of benefits and expanded opportunities. With the ability to hold two passports, individuals can enjoy greater mobility, access to improved healthcare and education, increased business prospects, and enhanced personal security. For those seeking to unlock these global opportunities, understanding the countries offering second passports becomes crucial.

This subchapter aims to provide a comprehensive overview of the countries that offer second passports and the benefits associated with each. It is essential to note that the acquisition of a second passport is a legal process, with each country having its own set of requirements and regulations. This guide will highlight some of the most popular options available to individuals seeking dual citizenship.

One of the prominent countries offering second passports is Malta. Known for its picturesque landscapes, rich history, and stable economy, Malta's citizenship program has gained immense popularity. By investing in the country's economy, individuals can obtain Maltese citizenship and enjoy visa-free access to over 180 countries, including the Schengen Zone.

Another sought-after option is Cyprus. The Cypriot citizenship-by-investment program presents an attractive opportunity for individuals looking to expand their global reach. With its strategic location, favorable tax regime, and access to the European Union, Cyprus offers a second passport that provides visa-free travel to over 170 countries.

For those seeking a Caribbean escape, the Commonwealth of Dominica offers an enticing citizenship-by-investment program. With its stunning natural beauty, political stability, and visa-free access to over 140 countries, Dominica's second passport provides individuals with an array of possibilities.

Other notable countries offering second passports include St. Kitts and Nevis, Grenada, and Antigua and Barbuda, all of which boast robust citizenship-by-investment programs. These nations provide individuals with the opportunity to obtain a second passport and enjoy the benefits of increased mobility, privacy, and access to global markets.

It is important to mention that the acquisition of a second passport should be approached with due diligence and professional guidance. Engaging the services of reputable firms specializing in citizenship-by-investment can ensure a smooth and compliant application process.

In conclusion, the world of second passports offers individuals unparalleled global opportunities. This subchapter has provided an overview of some of the countries offering second passports, highlighting their unique benefits and advantages. By exploring these options and seeking expert advice, individuals can unlock the potential of dual citizenship and open doors to a world of possibilities.

Comparison of Second Passport Programs

When considering obtaining a second passport, there are various programs available to cater to different needs and circumstances. This subchapter aims to provide an overview and comparison of different second passport programs, addressing the diverse audience of individuals seeking dual citizenship, passports for investment, diplomatic passports, high-security passports, passports for refugees and asylum seekers, temporary passports, passports for medical tourism, student passports, passports for digital nomads, and passports for retirees.

For those seeking dual citizenship, several countries offer attractive second-passure programs. These programs often require significant financial investments, such as real estate purchases, government bonds, or donations to national development funds. By comparing the costs, requirements, and benefits of these programs, individuals can make informed decisions that align with their financial capabilities and long-term goals.

Investors looking for citizenship by investment options will find that some countries have established programs aimed at attracting foreign investment. These programs provide a fast track to citizenship in exchange for substantial investments in the country's economy, such as job creation, infrastructure development, or financial contributions. By comparing the investment requirements, processing times, and privileges associated with each program, investors can select the option that best suits their investment strategy and objectives.

Government officials and diplomats may be interested in obtaining diplomatic passports to facilitate their roles in international affairs. This section will explore the requirements and benefits of diplomatic passports, including visa-free travel, diplomatic immunity, and access to consular services. It will also discuss the countries that offer diplomatic passports and the eligibility criteria for government officials and diplomats.

Individuals with high-risk occupations, such as journalists, aid workers, or security personnel, may require high-security passports to ensure their safety when traveling to volatile regions. This section will compare the security features, processing times, and validity periods of high-security passports offered by different countries, helping individuals choose the best option to meet their specific security needs.

The subchapter will also provide information on second passport programs designed for refugees and asylum seekers, temporary passports for business travelers or short-term expatriates, passports for medical tourism, student passports for international students studying abroad, passports for digital nomads or remote workers seeking alternative residency options, and passports for retirees seeking retirement havens or pensioner visas.

By offering a comprehensive comparison of second passport programs, this subchapter aims to empower the public with knowledge and insights to make informed decisions about their global opportunities and explore the potential of acquiring a second passport.

Chapter 3: Passports for Investment (Citizenship by Investment)

Overview of Citizenship by Investment Programs

Citizenship by investment programs, also known as economic citizenship programs or second passport programs, have gained significant popularity in recent years. These programs allow individuals to acquire citizenship in a foreign country by making a substantial investment in that country's economy. This subchapter will provide an overview of these programs and their various benefits and considerations.

For individuals seeking a second passport or dual citizenship, citizenship by investment programs offer a unique opportunity to obtain a new nationality and access a range of benefits. These programs provide a legal and legitimate way to obtain citizenship in a foreign country, allowing individuals to enjoy the rights and privileges associated with that citizenship. This can include visa-free travel to numerous countries, access to better healthcare and education systems, tax advantages, and increased business and investment opportunities.

Citizenship by investment programs varies from country to country, with each program having its own set of requirements and benefits. Some countries offer direct citizenship through investment, while others offer residency permits that can later lead to citizenship. The minimum investment required can range from a few hundred thousand dollars to several million, depending on the country and the investment options available.

The availability of citizenship by investment programs caters to a wide range of niches. For individuals in high-risk occupations, such as government officials, diplomats, or individuals involved in sensitive industries, acquiring a high-security passport through these programs can provide added security and protection. Refugees and asylum seekers can also benefit from these programs, as they offer an opportunity to obtain a new nationality and the associated rights and protections.

Additionally, citizenship by investment programs cater to other specific niches, such as business travelers, medical tourists, international students, digital nomads, and retirees seeking retirement havens. These programs provide alternative residency options, allowing individuals to explore new opportunities, access better healthcare or education, or enjoy a peaceful retirement in a foreign country.

However, it is essential to consider the potential drawbacks and risks associated with citizenship by investment programs. These programs have faced criticism for potentially facilitating money laundering or tax evasion, and individuals should carefully assess the reputation and credibility of the countries offering such programs. It is crucial to seek professional advice and thoroughly research the program requirements, investment options, and the long-term implications of obtaining citizenship through investment.

In conclusion, citizenship by investment programs offers a unique opportunity for individuals seeking a second passport or dual citizenship. These programs cater to various niches and provide access to a range of benefits. However, thorough research and professional guidance are essential to ensure individuals make informed decisions and understand the potential risks and implications associated with these programs.

Eligibility Criteria and Investment Options

When it comes to obtaining a second passport for dual citizenship, there are various eligibility criteria and investment options available to individuals from all walks of life. Whether you are a business traveler, retiree, student, government official, or someone with a high-risk occupation, there is a passport solution that suits your needs. In this subchapter, we will explore the different eligibility criteria and investment options for each niche.

For those seeking second passports for dual citizenship, the eligibility criteria often include having a certain level of wealth or investment in the country of interest. Many countries offer citizenship by investment programs, where individuals can make a significant financial contribution to the country's economy in exchange for citizenship. These programs typically require a minimum investment amount, which can vary depending on the country. By participating in these programs, individuals can obtain a second passport and enjoy the benefits of dual citizenship, including increased travel freedom and access to global opportunities.

Government officials and diplomats may be eligible for diplomatic passports, which provide special privileges and immunities while traveling abroad. These passports are typically issued to individuals who hold diplomatic positions or represent their countries internationally. High-security passports, on the other hand, are designed for individuals with high-risk occupations, such as journalists, aid workers, or security personnel. These passports offer enhanced security features and may provide additional protection while traveling to potentially dangerous areas.

Refugees and asylum seekers often face unique challenges when it comes to obtaining passports. Temporary passports may be available for these individuals, allowing them to travel internationally while their asylum status is being processed. Similarly, business travelers or short-term expatriates may benefit from temporary passports, which offer flexibility and convenience for frequent international travel.

For individuals seeking medical treatment abroad, medical tourism passports can provide a convenient solution. These passports may offer expedited visa processing or special medical assistance while traveling for medical purposes. International students studying abroad may also require student passports, which allow them to travel freely between their home country and their host country for educational purposes.

Digital nomads and remote workers looking for alternative residency options can explore passports that cater specifically to their needs. These passports may offer visa-free travel to popular digital nomad destinations or provide access to coworking spaces and other resources for remote workers.

Finally, retirees seeking retirement havens or pensioner visas can consider passports that offer attractive retirement benefits, such as tax advantages, healthcare access, and a high quality of life.

In conclusion, there are various eligibility criteria and investment options available for individuals seeking second passports for dual citizenship. Whether you are a government official, student, business traveler, or retiree, there is a passport solution tailored to your specific needs and goals. By exploring these options, individuals can unlock global opportunities and enjoy the benefits of alternative residency and citizenship.

Popular Countries with Citizenship by Investment Programs

As the world becomes increasingly globalized, the demand for second passports and dual citizenship has grown exponentially. This subchapter explores the popular countries that offer citizenship by investment programs, catering to a diverse range of individuals seeking to expand their global opportunities.

For those interested in second passports for dual citizenship, several countries stand out as attractive options. One such country is Malta, which offers a highly regarded citizenship program known as the Malta Individual Investor Program (MIIP). This program provides a fast-track route to Maltese citizenship for individuals who make a significant contribution to the country's economy.

Another popular choice is Cyprus, which offers the Cyprus Investment Program. This program allows individuals to obtain Cypriot citizenship through a variety of investment options, including real estate, government bonds, and business investment.

For high-net-worth individuals seeking diplomatic passports, countries like St. Kitts and Nevis offer their Citizenship by Investment Program. This program allows applicants to obtain citizenship in exchange for an investment in the country's economy, granting them the benefits and privileges of a diplomatic passport.

Individuals with high-risk occupations may find Grenada's Citizenship by Investment Program appealing. This program offers citizenship to those who invest in the country's economy, providing them with a high-security passport that allows for greater ease of travel.

For refugees and asylum seekers seeking a fresh start, countries like Portugal offer citizenship through investment programs that provide a pathway to legal residency and, ultimately, citizenship. These programs allow individuals to invest in the country's economy, providing them with a secure future and the benefits of a new passport.

Business travelers or short-term expatriates may find temporary passports offered by countries like Dominica to be a valuable asset. These passports allow for ease of travel and provide individuals with the flexibility to conduct business or explore opportunities abroad.

Students looking to study abroad can benefit from passports offered by countries like Ireland. These passports provide international students with the ability to travel and study in various countries, opening doors to educational and career opportunities.

Digital nomads and remote workers seeking alternative residency options may find countries like Estonia appealing. Estonia offers an e-residency program that provides individuals with a digital identity and the ability to conduct business remotely in the European Union.

Retirees seeking retirement havens or pensioner visas may find countries like Panama attractive. Panama offers a Friendly Nations Visa program, granting individuals residency and a pathway to citizenship through investment or pension income.

In conclusion, the world offers a wide range of countries with citizenship by investment programs that cater to different niches. Whether you are seeking second passports for dual citizenship, high-security passports, or alternative residency options, there are numerous opportunities available. By exploring these popular countries, individuals can unlock a world of global opportunities and expand their horizons.

Pros and Cons of Passport Investment Programs

Passport investment programs, also known as citizenship by investment, have gained significant popularity in recent years. These programs allow individuals to obtain a second passport by making a substantial financial contribution to a country's economy. While they offer various advantages, it is essential to consider the pros and cons before deciding to pursue such a program.

One of the significant benefits of passport investment programs is the opportunity to gain dual citizenship. Dual citizenship provides individuals with expanded travel and business opportunities, access to a broader range of healthcare and education options, and increased security and stability for their families. It also allows them to take advantage of tax planning strategies and diversify their assets globally.

For individuals in high-risk occupations or those seeking security, acquiring a second passport through investment programs can be a valuable asset. Diplomats, government officials, and individuals with high-risk occupations can benefit from the diplomatic immunity and high-security features that come with certain passports, ensuring their safety and freedom of movement.

Passport investment programs can also be advantageous for refugees and asylum seekers who are looking for a fresh start and a chance at a better life. These programs offer a pathway to legal status, protection, and access to the benefits and opportunities available in the host country.

However, it is essential to consider the drawbacks of passport investment programs as well. One of the main concerns is the potential for abuse and exploitation. Some critics argue that these programs can enable money laundering, tax evasion, and the entry of individuals with questionable backgrounds. It is crucial for countries offering such programs to have robust due diligence procedures in place to mitigate these risks.

Another consideration is the financial commitment required. Passport investment programs often require a significant investment, which may not be feasible for everyone. Additionally, there may be additional costs associated with maintaining the citizenship, such as annual fees or mandatory residence requirements.

Furthermore, obtaining a second passport through investment programs may not guarantee the same level of rights and privileges as native citizens. Some countries restrict certain rights, such as political participation, to individuals who acquire citizenship through investment programs.

In conclusion, passport investment programs offer a range of benefits, including dual citizenship, enhanced security, and expanded opportunities. However, it is crucial to carefully evaluate the pros and cons before deciding to pursue such a program. By considering the specific needs and goals of each individual, it is possible to make an informed decision that aligns with their unique circumstances and aspirations.

Chapter 4: Diplomatic Passports for Government Officials and Diplomats

Introduction to Diplomatic Passports

In today's globalized world, the concept of citizenship has expanded beyond mere nationality. Many individuals now seek to acquire second passports for various reasons, ranging from expanding their global opportunities to ensuring safety and security. This subchapter will provide an introduction to one specific type of second passport - the diplomatic passport.

Diplomatic passports are exclusively issued to government officials and diplomats, providing them with certain privileges and immunities while traveling abroad. These passports serve as a symbol of sovereignty and represent the authority and status of the individual carrying them.

For government officials and diplomats, diplomatic passports offer unparalleled benefits. They facilitate smooth travel and entry into foreign countries, often bypassing lengthy visa application processes. Diplomatic passport holders also enjoy diplomatic immunity, protecting them from arrest and prosecution in their host countries. This immunity extends to their immediate family members as well, ensuring their safety and security.

High-security features distinguish diplomatic passports from ordinary travel documents. These features include biometric data, tamper-proof materials, and advanced encryption technology. Such measures are essential for protecting sensitive information and preventing identity theft or fraudulent activities.

While diplomatic passports are primarily reserved for government officials and diplomats, they hold significance for individuals in other niches as well. Those engaged in high-risk occupations, such as journalists, aid workers, or business professionals operating in politically unstable regions, may benefit from the enhanced security features and diplomatic immunity offered by these passports.

In addition, diplomatic passports can also be utilized by individuals seeking alternative residency options. Digital nomads, remote workers, and retirees looking for retirement havens can explore the possibility of obtaining a diplomatic passport to facilitate their desired lifestyle or ensure their safety in foreign lands.

It is important to note that diplomatic passports are not available for purchase or through citizenship by investment programs. They are exclusively granted to individuals serving their respective governments in diplomatic capacities. However, this subchapter will provide valuable insights into the world of diplomatic passports and offer information on alternative options for those interested in second passports.

Whether you are a government official, diplomat, high-risk occupation professional, or seeking alternative residency options, understanding the benefits and limitations of diplomatic passports is crucial. This subchapter will serve as a gateway to unlocking the potential of diplomatic passports and exploring the broader realm of second passports for dual citizenship.

Benefits and Privileges of Diplomatic Passports

A diplomatic passport is a powerful tool that grants certain benefits and privileges to its holder. In this subchapter, we will explore the advantages that come with possessing a diplomatic passport, catering to a wide range of individuals, from government officials and diplomats to retirees seeking retirement havens.

For government officials and diplomats, a diplomatic passport is a symbol of their status and provides them with certain immunities and privileges. They enjoy diplomatic immunity, which means they are protected from prosecution and are exempt from certain taxes and customs duties. This immunity allows them to perform their duties effectively and without interference, ensuring the smooth functioning of diplomatic relations between countries.

Individuals with high-risk occupations, such as journalists or humanitarian workers, can benefit greatly from holding a diplomatic passport. It provides them with an added layer of security and protection when working in dangerous or volatile regions. In some cases, a diplomatic passport can help facilitate access to restricted areas and provide assistance from embassies or consulates in times of crisis.

For refugees and asylum seekers, a diplomatic passport can be a lifeline. It offers them a legal and recognized identity, which is crucial when seeking international protection and asylum. It allows them to travel safely and access consular assistance when needed.

Business travelers and short-term expatriates can benefit from temporary passports, which are often issued for the purpose of conducting business activities abroad. These passports provide flexibility and convenience, allowing individuals to travel and work internationally without the need for a long-term commitment.

Medical tourism is a growing industry, and individuals seeking medical treatment abroad can benefit from passports specifically designed for this purpose. These passports facilitate travel for medical purposes and may provide streamlined visa processes or access to specialized healthcare services.

International students studying abroad can also benefit from student passports. These passports often come with specific benefits, such as discounted travel fares or access to student services in foreign countries.

For digital nomads and remote workers who seek alternative residency options, some countries offer passports with specific privileges for this niche. These passports allow individuals to live and work remotely in different countries, tapping into the growing trend of location-independent employment.

Retirees seeking retirement havens or pensioner visas can also find value in diplomatic passports. Some countries offer retirement programs that provide special benefits and privileges, including access to healthcare services, tax incentives, and ease of travel.

In conclusion, diplomatic passports offer a range of benefits and privileges tailored to the specific needs of different individuals and niches. Whether you are a government official, a high-risk professional, a refugee, a student, a digital nomad, or a retiree, a diplomatic passport can open doors, offer protection, and enhance your global opportunities.

Application Process for Diplomatic Passports

Obtaining a diplomatic passport can open up a world of opportunities for government officials, diplomats, and individuals with high-risk occupations. This subchapter will guide you through the application process for diplomatic passports, providing valuable information for those seeking this prestigious travel document.

The application process for diplomatic passports varies from country to country, but there are general steps that most applicants must follow. Firstly, it is essential to establish your eligibility for a diplomatic passport. Typically, this requires being a government official, diplomat, or holding a high-ranking position in a recognized organization. It is important to note that diplomatic passports are not available to the general public.

Once you have determined your eligibility, the next step is to gather the necessary documents. These typically include a completed application form, proof of citizenship, a letter of appointment or employment, and a letter of recommendation from your superior or government department. Additionally, you may need to provide supporting documents such as a resume, educational certificates, and a valid travel itinerary.

After gathering the required documents, it is time to submit your application. This can usually be done either in person at the relevant government office or through an online application portal. It is important to carefully follow the instructions provided and ensure that all documents are correctly filled out and signed.

Once your application has been submitted, it will undergo a thorough review process. This may include background checks, security screenings, and verification of the information provided. The length of this process can vary depending on the country and the individual circumstances.

If your application is approved, you will be notified and invited to an appointment to finalize the process. This typically involves submitting additional documents, such as passport-sized photographs, paying the required fees, and taking an oath of allegiance.

Upon successful completion of the final steps, you will be issued a diplomatic passport. This powerful travel document grants you privileges and immunities while traveling abroad, including visa-free access to many countries and expedited entry and exit procedures.

In conclusion, the application process for diplomatic passports is a complex and thorough one. It requires careful attention to detail, a clear understanding of eligibility criteria, and the ability to provide supporting documents. If you are a government official, diplomat, or individual in a high-risk occupation, obtaining a diplomatic passport can greatly enhance your travel opportunities and provide you with a level of security and convenience not available to the general public.

Case Studies and Success Stories

In this subchapter, we will explore real-life case studies and success stories of individuals who have successfully obtained second passports for dual citizenship and navigated the complex process of acquiring alternative residency options. These inspiring stories will showcase the various niches that can benefit from dual citizenship and provide valuable insights and inspiration for those considering such opportunities.

First, we will delve into the world of passports for investment, also known as citizenship by investment programs. We will share the story of John, a successful entrepreneur who utilized this avenue to obtain a second passport, allowing him to expand his business globally and enjoy the benefits of international travel with ease.

Next, we will explore diplomatic passports for government officials and diplomats. Sarah, a seasoned diplomat, will share her journey of obtaining a diplomatic passport, enabling her to represent her country abroad and facilitate diplomatic relations on a global scale.

For individuals with high-risk occupations, we will highlight the importance of high-security passports. Alex, a journalist reporting from conflict zones, will recount the challenges he faced and how his high-security passport provided him with the necessary protection and access to continue his important work.

Passports for refugees and asylum seekers are another crucial aspect we will examine. We will introduce Anna, a refugee who successfully acquired a second passport, granting her the freedom and opportunities she longed for, ultimately shaping a brighter future for herself and her family.

In addition, we will showcase the significance of temporary passports for business travelers or short-term expatriates. Mark, a frequent business traveler, will share his experience of obtaining a temporary passport, allowing him to seamlessly conduct business internationally without unnecessary delays or complications.

Furthermore, we will explore passports for medical tourism. We will feature Linda, a patient seeking medical treatment abroad who utilized a second passport to access top-notch healthcare options and enjoy a comfortable recovery in a foreign country.

For international students studying abroad, we will present the success story of Jake, who obtained a student passport, enabling him to pursue his educational goals in a foreign country and immerse himself in a new culture.

Passports for digital nomads or remote workers looking for alternative residency options will also be covered. Emily, a digital nomad, will share her journey of acquiring a second passport, allowing her to work remotely from various countries and embrace the freedom of a location-independent lifestyle.

Lastly, we will explore passports for retirees seeking retirement havens or pensioner visas. William, a retiree, will recount his experience of obtaining a second passport and finding the perfect retirement haven that offers a high quality of life, healthcare benefits, and a welcoming environment for retirees.

These case studies and success stories demonstrate the immense value and life-changing opportunities that second passports for dual citizenship can offer across various niches. By unlocking global opportunities, individuals can broaden their horizons, enhance their lifestyles, and pursue their dreams on a global scale.

Chapter 5: High-Security Passports for Individuals with High-Risk Occupations

Understanding the Need for High-Security Passports

In today's increasingly interconnected world, the need for high-security passports has become more crucial than ever. As the global landscape continues to evolve, individuals from various walks of life find themselves in situations that demand a heightened level of security and protection. This subchapter aims to shed light on the significance of high-security passports for different niches, including second passports for dual citizenship, passports for investment, diplomatic passports for government officials and diplomats, and passports for individuals with high-risk occupations, among others.

For individuals seeking dual citizenship, a high-security passport offers peace of mind and enhanced global mobility. With the growing uncertainty in many regions, having the option to rely on a second passport provides an invaluable sense of security. Dual citizenship not only opens doors to new opportunities but also ensures access to essential services and protection in times of crisis.

Passports for investment, also known as citizenship by investment, have gained popularity among global investors. These passports offer a unique opportunity to combine economic growth with personal security. Investors can obtain a high-security passport by making a substantial investment in the country, contributing to its economic development while enjoying the privileges and protection that come with it.

Government officials and diplomats require diplomatic passports that afford them special privileges and immunities while representing their countries abroad. These high-security passports not only provide identification but also ensure the safety and protection of officials during their diplomatic missions.

Individuals engaged in high-risk occupations, such as journalists, aid workers, or security personnel, often face significant threats to their safety. High-security passports offer an added layer of protection, making it more challenging for malicious actors to forge or tamper with their travel documents. This heightened security can be a matter of life and death in some cases.

Refugees and asylum seekers, who often find themselves displaced and vulnerable, greatly benefit from high-security passports. These documents provide them with legitimate identification and facilitate their travel to safe havens, protecting them from exploitation and ensuring their rights are respected.

Temporary passports cater to the needs of business travelers and short-term expatriates. These high-security documents are designed for individuals who frequently travel for work purposes and require a reliable, secure means of identification during their trips.

Passports for medical tourism enable individuals to seek medical treatment abroad. These high-security documents ensure the privacy and protection of sensitive medical information, enabling patients to travel safely and access the best healthcare options worldwide.

International students studying abroad benefit from student passports, which provide secure identification and simplify the visa application process. These high-security passports allow students to focus on their education while enjoying the privileges and protections granted to them.

Digital nomads and remote workers seeking alternative residency options can obtain high-security passports that provide them with the flexibility to live and work in different countries. These documents offer a sense of stability, ensuring that their digital nomadic lifestyle is supported by secure identification and protection.

Lastly, retirees seeking retirement havens or pensioner visas can obtain high-security passports that grant them access to countries with favorable retirement conditions. These documents ensure the safety and security of retirees, granting them peace of mind as they embark on their new chapter in life.

In conclusion, high-security passports play a crucial role in meeting the unique needs and challenges faced by individuals in various niches. Whether it is for dual citizenship, investment purposes, diplomatic missions, high-risk occupations, or seeking refuge, these passports provide a sense of security, protection, and global mobility that is essential in today's rapidly changing world.

Features and Technologies of High-Security Passports

In today's rapidly changing world, the need for secure travel documents has become paramount. High-security passports are designed to protect individuals with high-risk occupations, government officials, diplomats, refugees, asylum seekers, and anyone seeking safe and hassle-free travel. They incorporate cutting-edge features and technologies that make them virtually tamper-proof and counterfeit-resistant. This subchapter explores the features and technologies that make high-security passports the ultimate travel document.

One of the key features of high-security passports is the use of biometric data. These passports include a microchip embedded with the holder's unique biometric information, such as fingerprints or iris scans. This technology ensures that the passport cannot be forged or used by anyone other than the legitimate holder.

Another important aspect is the use of advanced printing techniques. High-security passports employ specialized printing methods that make it extremely difficult to replicate or alter the document. These techniques include holographic foils, microprinting, and UV inks, which are nearly impossible to reproduce accurately.

Furthermore, high-security passports incorporate intricate designs and complex patterns that are visually appealing but also serve as anti-counterfeiting measures. These designs often include watermarks, guilloche patterns, and hidden images that can only be seen under certain lighting conditions.

In addition to these physical features, high-security passports also utilize encryption and digital signature technology. This ensures that the data stored in the passport's microchip is protected from unauthorized access or tampering. Encryption algorithms and secure protocols make it virtually impossible for hackers to compromise the integrity of the passport's data.

To further enhance security, high-security passports often come with additional features such as tamper-evident seals, invisible UV markings, and laser-engraved personalization. These features make it easy to identify if the passport has been tampered with or forged.

High-security passports are not only limited to government officials or diplomats; they are also available for individuals seeking alternative residency options, retirees, and students studying abroad. These passports offer peace of mind and a higher level of security for those who require it.

In conclusion, high-security passports incorporate a range of features and technologies that provide individuals with the utmost protection and security during their travels. These passports are designed to be resistant to forgery, tampering, and unauthorized use. Whether you are a government official, a high-risk occupation worker, a student, or a retiree, a high-security passport ensures that your travel documents are legitimate, secure, and reliable.

Countries Offering High-Security Passports

In today's globalized world, having a strong and secure passport can open up a world of opportunities. Whether you are seeking dual citizenship, exploring investment options, or looking for alternative residency, a high-security passport can provide you with the peace of mind and freedom to travel without unnecessary risks. In this subchapter, we will explore the countries that offer high-security passports, ensuring the safety and protection of individuals in various circumstances.

For individuals with high-risk occupations, such as journalists, aid workers, or business professionals working in conflict zones, certain countries offer passports with advanced security features. These features include biometric data, encrypted chips, and tamper-proof technology, making it extremely difficult for unauthorized individuals to forge or tamper with the passport.

Moreover, countries like Germany, Canada, and Australia offer high-security passports to government officials and diplomats. These passports come with additional privileges, including diplomatic immunity and enhanced protection while traveling abroad on official business.

For individuals seeking a second passport through investment, several countries offer citizenship through investment programs. These programs allow individuals to obtain a high-security passport by making a significant investment in the country's economy. Countries like Malta, Cyprus, and St. Kitts and Nevis offer such programs, providing individuals with the opportunity to secure a second citizenship and a high-security passport.

Additionally, countries like Canada, Germany, and the United States offer refugee and asylum seekers the opportunity to obtain high-security passports, ensuring their safety and protection as they seek a new life in a foreign land.

For business travelers or short-term expatriates, some countries offer temporary passports with advanced security features. These passports are designed to provide individuals with a secure travel document for a limited period, making it convenient for frequent travelers.

Medical tourism has become increasingly popular, with individuals traveling abroad for specialized medical treatments. Countries like India, Thailand, and Singapore offer high-security passports to cater to the growing demand for medical tourism, ensuring the safety and protection of travelers.

International students studying abroad can also benefit from high-security passports. Countries like the United Kingdom, Canada, and Australia offer student passports with advanced security features, ensuring the safety and protection of students as they pursue their education in a foreign country.

Furthermore, for digital nomads or remote workers seeking alternative residency options, countries like Estonia and Barbados offer high-security passports that cater to the unique needs of this niche. These passports provide individuals with the flexibility to work and live abroad while enjoying the benefits of a secure travel document.

Lastly, retirees seeking retirement havens or pensioner visas can obtain high-security passports in countries like Panama, Costa Rica, and Portugal. These passports provide retirees with the peace of mind and security they need as they embark on a new chapter in their lives.

In conclusion, having a high-security passport is essential for individuals in various circumstances. Whether you are seeking dual citizenship, investing in a foreign country, or pursuing alternative residency options, several countries offer high-security passports that ensure your safety, protection, and freedom to explore global opportunities.

Ensuring the Confidentiality of High-Security Passports

In today's interconnected world, the need for secure and confidential travel documents has never been more crucial. High-security passports provide individuals with the peace of mind they need when traveling abroad, especially for those with high-risk occupations, government officials, diplomats, and individuals seeking refuge or asylum. This subchapter will delve into the measures taken to ensure the confidentiality of these passports, catering to a diverse audience ranging from dual citizenship seekers to retirees seeking retirement havens.

High-security passports are designed with multiple layers of protection to safeguard personal information and prevent unauthorized access. Advanced printing techniques, such as holograms, microprinting, and UV imaging, are employed to make counterfeiting nearly impossible. In addition, embedded chips containing biometric information further enhance the security of these passports, ensuring that only the authorized individual can access their data.

To ensure the confidentiality of high-security passports, stringent protocols are followed during the application and processing stages. Extensive background checks, including criminal record checks and verification of identity, are conducted to confirm the applicant's eligibility for a high-security passport. This rigorous screening process minimizes the risk of issuing passports to individuals with malicious intent and ensures the integrity of the passport system.

Furthermore, governments and passport issuing authorities have implemented robust data protection measures to safeguard the personal information of passport holders. Encryption techniques are employed to secure data stored within the embedded chips, making it extremely difficult for unauthorized individuals to access or alter the information. Regular audits and security assessments are conducted to identify and address any vulnerabilities in the passport system, ensuring that it remains resilient against emerging threats.

It is important to note that the confidentiality of high-security passports goes beyond the physical document itself. Governments and passport issuers are committed to maintaining the privacy of passport holders' information, adhering to strict data protection regulations. Personal data is stored in secure databases and is only accessed by authorized personnel for legitimate purposes. Measures are in place to prevent unauthorized disclosure or misuse of personal information, providing individuals with the assurance that their privacy is respected and protected.

In conclusion, ensuring the confidentiality of high-security passports is of utmost importance in today's global landscape. By incorporating advanced printing techniques, biometric data, rigorous screening processes, and robust data protection measures, individuals can trust that their personal information is secure and confidential. Whether you are a high-risk professional, a government official, a student studying abroad, or a retiree seeking a retirement haven, high-security passports offer the peace of mind you need to confidently explore global opportunities.

Chapter 6: Passports for Refugees and Asylum Seekers

The Challenges Faced by Refugees and Asylum Seekers

Introduction:

In today's tumultuous world, millions of individuals are forced to leave their homes due to conflicts, persecution, or other forms of violence. These individuals, known as refugees and asylum seekers, face numerous challenges in their quest for safety and a better future. This subchapter will shed light on the challenges faced by refugees and asylum seekers and explore potential solutions to alleviate their hardships.

1. Legal and Administrative Hurdles:

One of the biggest challenges for refugees and asylum seekers is navigating the complex legal and administrative processes of seeking asylum. They often encounter language barriers, limited access to legal aid, and unfamiliarity with the host country's legal system. This can result in delays, rejection of asylum claims, or even deportation back to dangerous conditions.

2. Discrimination and Stigmatization:

Refugees and asylum seekers often face discrimination and stigmatization in their host countries. They may be perceived as a burden on resources, potential security risks, or simply unwanted outsiders. This prejudice can lead to limited access to education, healthcare, employment, and housing, exacerbating their vulnerability and hindering their integration into society.

3. Psychological Trauma and Mental Health:

The journey of fleeing one's homeland and seeking asylum is often traumatic, leaving refugees and asylum seekers with deep psychological scars. They may have witnessed or experienced violence, loss of loved ones, or displacement. Access to mental health support is crucial to help them overcome these challenges and rebuild their lives.

4. Socio-economic Integration:

Finding employment and achieving socio-economic stability is a significant challenge for refugees and asylum seekers. Language barriers, unrecognized qualifications or work experience, and prejudice from employers can make it difficult for them to secure meaningful employment. This perpetuates their dependence on welfare systems and hinders their ability to contribute to the host country's economy.

5. Family Separation and Unaccompanied Minors:

Many refugees and asylum seekers are forced to leave their families behind or become separated during their journey. This separation causes immense emotional distress and uncertainty. Unaccompanied minors face additional challenges, as they are particularly vulnerable to exploitation, trafficking, and limited access to education and protection.

Conclusion:

The challenges faced by refugees and asylum seekers are multifaceted and require comprehensive solutions. Governments, international organizations, and civil society must work together to address the legal, social, and economic barriers that hinder their integration and well-being. Providing accessible legal aid, combating discrimination, prioritizing mental health support, promoting socio-economic integration, and ensuring family reunification are crucial steps towards empowering refugees and asylum seekers to rebuild their lives and contribute positively to their host communities.

International Laws and Protocols on Refugee Status

Refugees and asylum seekers face numerous challenges when seeking safety and a better life in a foreign country. To ensure their protection and fair treatment, international laws and protocols have been established to address the specific needs and rights of individuals fleeing persecution or conflict. This subchapter explores the key international laws and protocols on refugee status, providing valuable information for various audiences, including those interested in second passports for dual citizenship, passports for refugees and asylum seekers, and passports for retirees seeking retirement havens or pensioner visas.

The 1951 United Nations Convention Relating to the Status of Refugees is the cornerstone of international refugee protection. It defines a refugee as someone who, due to a well-founded fear of being persecuted for reasons of race, religion, nationality, membership of a particular social group, or political opinion, is outside their home country and cannot return. This convention also outlines the rights and obligations of both refugees and the countries that host them.

In addition to the convention, the 1967 Protocol Relating to the Status of Refugees expanded the scope of protection to include individuals who became refugees after 1951. This ensures that refugees are not left unprotected if they were displaced after the convention was adopted.

The principle of non-refoulment, a fundamental norm in refugee law, prohibits the return of refugees to a country where they would face persecution or serious harm. This principle is enshrined in various international human rights treaties and customary international law, providing a crucial safeguard for refugees.

Furthermore, the work of the United Nations High Commissioner for Refugees (UNHCR) plays a vital role in protecting and assisting refugees worldwide. The UNHCR works with governments, NGOs, and other stakeholders to ensure that refugees receive the necessary support, including access to education, healthcare, and legal assistance.

For individuals interested in second passports for dual citizenship or passports for refugees and asylum seekers, understanding these international laws and protocols is crucial. By knowing these laws, individuals can make informed decisions about their legal status and seek appropriate channels for protection and support.

Overall, this subchapter provides an overview of the international laws and protocols on refugee status, emphasizing their importance for various audiences, including those seeking second passports, individuals fleeing persecution, and retirees seeking retirement havens. By understanding these laws, individuals can navigate the complex landscape of refugee protection and work towards a better future for themselves and their families.

Countries Providing Passports for Refugees and Asylum Seekers

In the world we live in today, millions of people are forced to leave their homes due to conflict, persecution, or other forms of violence. These individuals, known as refugees and asylum seekers, often face tremendous challenges in their search for safety and a better life. One crucial aspect of their journey is obtaining a passport that grants them the right to travel and seek protection in another country.

Fortunately, several countries around the world recognize the plight of refugees and asylum seekers and offer them the opportunity to obtain passports. These passports not only provide them with the freedom to travel but also grant them certain rights and protections.

One such country is Canada. Known for its commitment to human rights and refugee protection, Canada offers refugees and asylum seekers the opportunity to obtain a refugee travel document (RTD).

This document allows them to travel internationally and serves as a valid form of identification in many countries. Canada's RTD is recognized under the Geneva Convention on Refugees, ensuring that refugees can travel safely and seek protection wherever they may go.

Another country that provides passports for refugees and asylum seekers is Germany. Germany offers a refugee passport to individuals who have been granted asylum or subsidiary protection in the country. This passport allows them to travel internationally and provides them with certain rights and benefits, including access to healthcare and social services.

Sweden is also known for its generous policies towards refugees and asylum seekers. The country offers a travel document to individuals who have been granted a residence permit on humanitarian grounds. This document allows them to travel internationally and provides them with a sense of security and stability.

These are just a few examples of countries that recognize the importance of providing passports to refugees and asylum seekers. By granting them the right to travel and seek protection, these countries are not only fulfilling their international obligations but also empowering individuals to rebuild their lives and contribute to society.

It is important to note that the process of obtaining a passport as a refugee or asylum seeker may vary from country to country. However, organizations such as the United Nations High Commissioner for Refugees (UNHCR) and local refugee support groups can provide valuable assistance and guidance throughout the application process.

In conclusion, passports for refugees and asylum seekers play a crucial role in providing them with the freedom to travel and seek protection. Countries such as Canada, Germany, and Sweden recognize the importance of offering these individuals a pathway to a better life. By doing so, they are not only fulfilling their humanitarian obligations but also creating opportunities for refugees and asylum seekers to thrive and contribute to their new communities.

Supportive Organizations and Resources

Obtaining a second passport for dual citizenship or exploring other passport options can seem like a daunting task. However, there are numerous supportive organizations and resources available to guide you through the process and make it as smooth as possible. Whether you are seeking a second passport for investment purposes, diplomatic reasons, or personal circumstances, these organizations can provide valuable assistance and information tailored to your specific needs.

For individuals interested in second passports for dual citizenship, organizations such as Global Citizenship Solutions and Dual Citizenships International offer comprehensive services to help you navigate the complex legal requirements and documentation needed. These organizations have extensive knowledge and experience in this area, guiding eligibility criteria, application procedures, and potential investment options.

Passports for investment, also known as citizenship by investment programs, are becoming increasingly popular. The International Investor Immigration Council and the Investment Migration Council are reputable organizations that specialize in this niche. They can provide you with up-to-date information on countries offering citizenship by investment programs, including the investment requirements, benefits, and potential pitfalls to be aware of.

Government officials and diplomats requiring diplomatic passports can turn to organizations like the International Civil Service Commission and the United Nations for guidance. These organizations can provide information on the diplomatic passport application process, requirements, and privileges associated with diplomatic status.

Individuals with high-risk occupations, such as journalists, aid workers, or security personnel, may benefit from organizations like the International Organization for Migration and Reporters Without Borders. These organizations can provide support and resources to ensure the safety and security of individuals working in volatile environments.

For refugees and asylum seekers, organizations like the United Nations High Commissioner for Refugees (UNHCR) and Amnesty International offer invaluable support. They guide the asylum application process, legal rights, and access to resources for those seeking protection and assistance.

Business travelers or short-term expatriates in need of temporary passports can rely on organizations like the International Air Transport Association (IATA) and the International Civil Aviation Organization (ICAO). These organizations can provide information on travel document requirements, visa regulations, and other essential travel-related resources.

For individuals seeking medical tourism opportunities abroad, organizations like the Medical Tourism Association and the International Medical Travel Journal can guide them on obtaining passports for medical purposes, as well as information on reputable healthcare facilities and destinations.

International students studying abroad can benefit from organizations like the Institute of International Education and the Association of International Educators. These organizations offer resources on student visa applications, scholarships, and cultural exchange programs.

Digital nomads or remote workers looking for alternative residency options can turn to organizations such as the Digital Nomad Association and Remote Year. These organizations provide information on countries offering digital nomad visas, co-working spaces, and communities tailored to the needs of location-independent professionals.

Retirees seeking retirement havens or pensioner visas can rely on organizations like Live and Invest Overseas and International Living. These organizations offer insights into countries with favorable retirement programs, including information on visa requirements, healthcare services, and lifestyle considerations.

In conclusion, supportive organizations and resources play a crucial role in assisting individuals in their pursuit of second passports, citizenship by investment, diplomatic passports, and various other passport options. By leveraging the expertise and guidance provided by these organizations, individuals can navigate the complexities of the application process with confidence and ease.

Chapter 7: Temporary Passports for Business Travelers or Short-Term Expatriates

Overview of Temporary Passports

In today's globalized world, the need for international travel has become increasingly common. Whether you are a business traveler, a student studying abroad, a government official, or simply seeking alternative residency options, having a passport that allows you to travel freely is crucial. This subchapter aims to provide an overview of temporary passports, their benefits, and the specific niches they cater to.

Temporary passports are a valuable tool for individuals who require short-term travel documents for various purposes. They are particularly useful for business travelers or short-term expatriates who need to make frequent trips to work. These passports offer flexibility and convenience, allowing individuals to travel without the lengthy process of obtaining full-fledged citizenship or long-term residency.

For those seeking medical treatment abroad, temporary passports can be a game-changer. Medical tourism has gained popularity in recent years, with individuals traveling to other countries to receive high-quality healthcare at a fraction of the cost. Temporary passports facilitate these journeys, allowing patients to access medical facilities and return to their home country once treatment is complete.

International students studying abroad also benefit from temporary passports. These documents enable students to pursue their education in foreign countries, experience new cultures, and gain a global perspective. Temporary passports simplify the visa application process, ensuring that students can focus on their studies rather than bureaucratic procedures.

Digital nomads and remote workers looking for alternative residency options can also take advantage of temporary passports. These individuals often seek the freedom to work and live in different countries without the limitations of traditional employment. Temporary passports provide the necessary documentation to explore new locations and take advantage of unique professional opportunities.

Retirees seeking retirement havens or pensioner visas can benefit from temporary passports as well. Many countries offer attractive retirement programs, granting special visas to retirees who meet specific criteria. Temporary passports facilitate this transition, allowing retirees to enjoy their golden years in a new and exciting environment.

In conclusion, temporary passports offer a range of benefits for various niches, including business travelers, medical tourists, students, digital nomads, retirees, and more. These passports provide individuals with the necessary documentation and flexibility to explore new opportunities, whether it be for work, education, healthcare, or retirement. By understanding the advantages of temporary passports, individuals can unlock global opportunities and experience the world in an unprecedented way.

Benefits and Limitations of Temporary Passports

In today's increasingly globalized world, the need for temporary passports has become more prevalent than ever before. Temporary passports serve a specific purpose for various individuals, including business travelers, short-term expatriates, and those seeking medical treatment abroad, among others. This subchapter aims to explore the benefits and limitations of temporary passports, catering to the diverse needs of the public across different niches.

For business travelers or short-term expatriates, temporary passports offer a range of advantages. Firstly, they provide a convenient and time-efficient solution for individuals who frequently travel for business purposes. Temporary passports can be obtained swiftly, allowing professionals to embark on their trips without delay. Furthermore, these passports often offer expedited processing at immigration checkpoints, thereby reducing wait times and enhancing the overall travel experience.

Temporary passports also come with certain limitations, primarily related to their validity period. As the name suggests, these passports are valid for a limited duration, typically ranging from a few months to a year. This restricts the duration of stay in a foreign country and may require frequent passport renewals for individuals who frequently travel. Additionally, temporary passports may not provide the same level of privileges and benefits as regular passports, such as visa-free travel to certain countries.

Another niche that benefits from temporary passports is medical tourism. Individuals seeking medical treatment abroad can obtain temporary passports to facilitate their travel and ensure smooth access to healthcare services. These passports enable patients to receive specialized medical care in foreign countries, often at a more affordable cost or with higher quality standards. Temporary passports for medical tourism allow individuals to explore a wider range of treatment options and access advanced medical technologies not available in their home countries.

However, it is important to acknowledge that temporary passports also have limitations within the realm of medical tourism. The duration of validity and the specific countries covered by these passports may vary, potentially limiting the scope of medical treatment options available to patients. Additionally, temporary passports may not grant the same rights and privileges as regular passports, such as access to emergency medical services or repatriation benefits in case of unforeseen circumstances.

In conclusion, temporary passports cater to the diverse needs of individuals across various niches, offering numerous benefits while also presenting certain limitations. Whether it is for business travel, medical tourism, or other temporary endeavors, these passports provide a valuable solution for those seeking short-term international mobility. However, individuals must carefully consider the duration of validity and specific limitations associated with temporary passports to make informed decisions regarding their travel plans and requirements.

Applying for Temporary Passports

In today's increasingly globalized world, individuals from all walks of life are seeking opportunities abroad. Whether you are a business traveler, a student studying abroad, or a retiree seeking a new haven, having the right passport can open doors to a world of possibilities. This subchapter focuses on the process of applying for temporary passports, catering to a diverse range of individuals seeking short-term residency or travel options.

For business travelers or short-term expatriates, temporary passports provide the flexibility and convenience needed to navigate the global business landscape. These passports typically offer shorter validity periods and are designed to meet the specific needs of individuals traveling for work or short-term assignments. We delve into the application process, providing step-by-step guidance on gathering the necessary documents, completing the application forms, and understanding the specific requirements for each country.

Additionally, we explore the unique needs of individuals seeking passports for medical tourism. Medical advancements and specialized treatments have made traveling abroad for medical purposes a popular choice. Temporary passports can facilitate this process by ensuring smooth travel arrangements and providing the necessary documentation for medical treatments overseas. We offer valuable insights into the application process, highlighting the key considerations and requirements for obtaining a temporary passport for medical tourism.

Furthermore, we address the needs of international students studying abroad. Studying in a foreign country can be an enriching experience, but it also comes with its own set of challenges. Temporary passports specifically tailored for students can streamline the visa application process and provide a sense of security and ease during their time abroad. We provide comprehensive guidance on the application process, including the necessary supporting documents and visa requirements for students.

Lastly, we discuss the benefits of temporary passports for digital nomads, remote workers, and retirees seeking alternative residency options. These individuals often yearn for flexibility, freedom, and the ability to explore new destinations while maintaining their professional or retired status. Temporary passports can offer the perfect solution, granting access to various countries without the need for long-term commitments. We outline the application process, highlighting the unique requirements and advantages of this niche group.

No matter your reason for seeking a temporary passport, this subchapter aims to demystify the application process and equip you with the knowledge needed to unlock global opportunities. With our comprehensive guidance, you will be well-prepared to embark on your journey and make the most of your temporary residency or travel abroad.

Traveling with Temporary Passports - Tips and Recommendations

For many individuals, traveling with temporary passports can be a necessity for various reasons, such as business trips, short-term exile, or even emergencies. While temporary passports may not offer the same benefits and privileges as regular passports, they are essential documents that can help facilitate international travel. In this subchapter, we will explore some valuable tips and recommendations for individuals traveling with temporary passports.

1. Understand the limitations: Temporary passports are issued for a limited period and often have restrictions on their usage. It is crucial to familiarize yourself with the specific limitations associated with your temporary passport, such as restricted countries or reduced visa-free access. This knowledge will help you plan your travel accordingly and avoid any unnecessary complications.

2. Check visa requirements: As a temporary passport holder, you may need to obtain visas for certain countries that offer visa-free access to regular passport holders. Before embarking on your journey, thoroughly research the visa requirements for your destination countries and ensure you have ample time to complete the application process.

3. Carry necessary supporting documents: To mitigate any potential issues at immigration checkpoints, it is advisable to carry supporting documents that can establish your identity, purpose of travel, and financial stability. These may include copies of your birth certificate, proof of employment or business ties, bank statements, and travel itineraries.

4. Maintain contact with your embassy or consulate: Temporary passport holders should always be aware of the contact details and location of their home country's embassy or consulate in the destination country. In case of any emergencies or issues, they can provide valuable assistance and guidance.

5. Purchase travel insurance: Temporary passport holders are often more vulnerable to unforeseen circumstances during their travels. It is highly recommended to invest in comprehensive travel insurance that covers medical emergencies, trip cancellations, and lost belongings. This will provide you with peace of mind and financial protection throughout your journey.

6. Keep your temporary passport secure: Since temporary passports are valid for a limited period, losing or misplacing them can cause significant inconvenience. Take extra precautions to keep your passport secure at all times, such as using a money belt, keeping a digital copy, and storing it separately from other valuables.

By following these tips and recommendations, individuals traveling with temporary passports can ensure a smoother and hassle-free travel experience. While temporary passports may not offer the same privileges as regular passports, they are valuable documents that enable individuals to fulfill their travel requirements efficiently.

Chapter 8: Passports for Medical Tourism (Traveling Abroad for Medical Treatment)

Introduction to Medical Tourism and Passport Requirements

In recent years, medical tourism has gained popularity as an alternative option for individuals seeking high-quality healthcare services at affordable prices. This subchapter aims to provide an introduction to medical tourism and the passport requirements associated with it. Whether you are considering traveling abroad for medical treatment or simply interested in understanding this growing phenomenon, this guide will equip you with the necessary knowledge.

Medical tourism involves traveling to another country to receive medical treatment, typically due to cost considerations, wait times, or the unavailability of certain procedures in one's home country. This practice has become more accessible and attractive to individuals from various backgrounds, including those seeking second passports for dual citizenship, passports for investment, and even diplomats or government officials in need of diplomatic passports. Additionally, high-security passports may be essential for individuals with high-risk occupations, while refugees, asylum seekers, and temporary business travelers may also require specific passport arrangements.

When it comes to medical tourism, having the appropriate passport is crucial. Different countries have varying passport requirements for medical travelers, such as visa requirements, validity periods, and the need for additional documentation. This subchapter will delve into these requirements, ensuring that you are well-prepared for your medical journey.

Moreover, this subchapter recognizes the diverse needs of individuals seeking medical treatment abroad. Whether you are a student studying abroad, a digital nomad or remote worker seeking residency options, or a retiree looking for retirement havens or pensioner visas, we will explore how medical tourism can cater to your specific circumstances. By understanding the passport requirements associated with these niches, you can make informed decisions regarding your healthcare options.

Unlocking Global Opportunities: A Guide to Second Passports for Dual Citizenship aims to provide comprehensive information for individuals interested in exploring medical tourism. This subchapter will serve as a starting point, equipping you with the necessary knowledge to navigate the world of medical tourism and understand the passport requirements associated with it.

In the following chapters, we will delve deeper into the various aspects of medical tourism, including destination choices, healthcare quality assessments, and legal considerations. By the end of this guide, you will have a holistic understanding of medical tourism and the passport requirements necessary to embark on this transformative journey.

Remember, your health is your most valuable asset, and with the right passport in hand, you can unlock a world of global opportunities for your medical needs. Let us embark on this journey together and discover the potential of medical tourism for your well-being.

Countries Recognized for Medical Tourism

Medical tourism, the practice of traveling abroad for medical treatment, has become increasingly popular in recent years. Many individuals are seeking high-quality healthcare options at more affordable prices, and several countries have stepped up to meet this growing demand. In this subchapter, we will explore some of the countries recognized for medical tourism and the benefits they offer to patients from around the world.

1. Thailand: Known for its world-class hospitals and highly trained medical professionals, Thailand has emerged as a leader in medical tourism. The country offers a wide range of procedures, from cosmetic surgery to complex heart surgeries, at a fraction of the cost in other countries.

2. India: With its advanced medical infrastructure, India has become a hub for medical tourists seeking affordable and high-quality treatment. The country is renowned for its expertise in procedures such as organ transplants, orthopedic surgeries, and cancer treatments.

3. Singapore: Singapore is known for its cutting-edge technology and excellent healthcare facilities. It attracts medical tourists seeking specialized treatments like neurology, cardiology, and oncology. The country also offers a seamless patient experience with its efficient healthcare system.

4. Malaysia: Malaysia has gained recognition for its affordable yet world-class healthcare services. The country is particularly popular for medical tourists seeking dental procedures, fertility treatments, and cosmetic surgeries.

5. Mexico: Mexico has become a popular destination for individuals from the United States seeking affordable healthcare options. The country offers a range of medical services, including dental care, weight loss surgeries, and cosmetic procedures.

6. Costa Rica: Costa Rica is known for its high-quality healthcare system and affordable medical treatments. The country is a preferred destination for medical tourists seeking dental work, cosmetic surgeries, and orthopedic procedures.

7. South Korea: South Korea has gained a reputation for its advanced cosmetic and plastic surgery options. The country offers innovative procedures, including facial contouring, double eyelid surgery, and liposuction.

These are just a few examples of the countries recognized for medical tourism. Each country offers its unique advantages, such as cost savings, high-quality healthcare, and cutting-edge technology. It is important for individuals considering medical tourism to research and choose a destination that best suits their specific needs and requirements.

Medical tourism has opened up a world of opportunities for individuals seeking affordable and high-quality healthcare. Whether you are in need of a routine procedure or a complex surgery, exploring the options available in these recognized countries can provide you with a cost-effective and reliable solution. Remember to consult with medical professionals and do thorough research before making any decisions regarding your medical treatment abroad.

Obtaining Passports for Medical Tourism

Traveling abroad for medical treatment, also known as medical tourism, has become increasingly popular in recent years. The opportunity to combine high-quality healthcare with a vacation in a foreign country has attracted many individuals seeking specialized treatments, lower costs, or shorter waiting times. This subchapter explores the process of obtaining passports specifically for medical tourism, providing valuable information for those considering this option.

When it comes to medical tourism, having a valid passport is crucial. In this subchapter, we will discuss the necessary steps and requirements for obtaining a passport for medical purposes. Whether you are seeking elective surgeries, specialized treatments, or alternative therapies, understanding the passport application process is essential to ensure a smooth journey.

The first step in obtaining a passport for medical tourism is to gather the required documentation. This usually includes a valid identification document, such as a birth certificate or national ID card, proof of citizenship, and proof of medical treatment or consultation abroad. It is important to research the specific requirements of the destination country, as some may have additional documentation requirements.

Next, it is advisable to consult with a travel agent or specialized medical tourism agency. These professionals can guide you through the application process and help you navigate any potential challenges. They can also provide valuable insights into the medical facilities, treatments, and accommodations available in your chosen destination.

For individuals seeking passports for medical tourism, it is important to consider the duration of the treatment and the potential need for multiple visits. Some countries offer special visa categories or temporary passports specifically designed for medical tourists. These options may allow for longer stays or multiple entries, making it easier to complete the necessary treatments.

Finally, it is essential to consider the financial aspects of medical tourism and the associated costs. In many cases, medical treatments abroad can be more affordable than in one's home country. However, it is crucial to factor in the cost of travel, accommodation, and post-treatment care. Understanding the financial implications will help you plan your medical tourism journey effectively.

In conclusion, obtaining a passport for medical tourism is a crucial step for those seeking healthcare abroad. By understanding the documentation requirements, consulting with professionals, and considering the financial aspects, individuals can ensure a smooth and successful medical tourism experience. Whether you are seeking specialized treatments, cost savings, or shorter waiting times, a passport for medical tourism opens up a world of opportunities for those in need of medical care.

Insurance and Legal Considerations for Medical Tourists

Medical tourism, the act of traveling abroad for medical treatment, has become increasingly popular in recent years. People are seeking high-quality and affordable healthcare options outside their home countries, and this trend has created a need for comprehensive insurance and legal considerations for medical tourists. In this subchapter, we will explore the various aspects of insurance and legal considerations that medical tourists should be aware of before embarking on their journey.

One of the primary concerns for medical tourists is insurance coverage. It is crucial to have adequate health insurance that covers medical treatments abroad. Depending on the destination country, healthcare costs may vary significantly, and without proper insurance, medical tourists can face exorbitant expenses. Additionally, insurance policies should also cover any potential complications or follow-up treatments that may be required after returning home.

In the context of legal considerations, medical tourists must be aware of the legal framework and regulations in the destination country. They should thoroughly research the country's healthcare system, licensing requirements for medical professionals, and the legal recourse available in case of medical malpractice or other mishaps. Engaging the services of a reputable medical tourism facilitator can help navigate the legal aspects and ensure a smooth and hassle-free experience.

Furthermore, medical tourists should also consider the legal implications of traveling with medications or medical devices.

Different countries have varying regulations regarding the importation of prescription drugs and medical equipment. It is essential to understand these regulations and obtain the necessary permits or documentation to avoid any legal complications while traveling.

Another crucial aspect to consider is the liability of the medical tourism facility or healthcare provider. Medical tourists should inquire about the facility's liability insurance coverage and seek legal advice to understand their rights and recourse in case of any medical negligence or malpractice.

Finally, medical tourists should also evaluate the potential risks associated with traveling for medical treatment. This includes considering the political stability and safety of the destination country, as well as the accessibility of emergency medical care.

In conclusion, insurance and legal considerations are of paramount importance for medical tourists. Having comprehensive health insurance coverage, understanding the legal framework, and assessing potential risks are essential steps in ensuring a safe and successful medical tourism experience. By being well-informed and prepared, medical tourists can make informed decisions and have peace of mind throughout their journey.

Chapter 9: Student Passports for International Students Studying Abroad

Importance of Student Passports for International Students

In today's globalized world, pursuing higher education abroad has become an increasingly popular choice for students seeking a well-rounded education and expanded opportunities. As such, obtaining a student passport has become an essential tool for international students. This subchapter aims to shed light on the significance of student passports for international students and the benefits they provide.

A student passport serves as a gateway to a world of educational possibilities. It enables international students to study in foreign countries, experience diverse cultures, and gain valuable insights into different academic systems. With a student passport, students can pursue their desired academic programs without the restrictions imposed by their home countries. This allows them to access a wider range of educational institutions renowned for their excellence in specific fields of study.

Moreover, possessing a student passport grants international students the ability to travel freely to and from their host countries. This freedom of movement allows students to explore nearby cities, countries, and landmarks, enhancing their cultural understanding and personal growth. It also facilitates participation in academic conferences, internships, and exchange programs, maximizing their learning opportunities and networking potential.

Another crucial aspect of student passports is the access they provide to various scholarships, grants, and financial aid programs exclusively available to international students. Many countries and institutions offer funding opportunities specifically designed to support the education of international students. These scholarships can significantly ease the financial burden on students and enable them to pursue their academic goals with peace of mind.

Furthermore, possessing a student passport instills a sense of independence, self-reliance, and adaptability in international students. Living and studying in a foreign country can be a transformative experience, fostering personal growth, cross-cultural communication skills, and a global perspective. Employers highly value these qualities in today's competitive job market, as they demonstrate a student's ability to navigate diverse environments and work effectively with people from different backgrounds.

In conclusion, student passports play a vital role in facilitating educational journeys for international students. They open doors to world-class educational institutions, provide freedom of movement, grant access to financial aid opportunities, and foster personal and professional growth. As such, obtaining a student passport is an invaluable step for any student aspiring to study abroad and unlock the global opportunities that await them.

Applying for Student Passports

If you are an international student seeking to study abroad, obtaining a student passport is an essential step in your journey towards higher education. A student passport not only permits you to study in another country but also provides various benefits and opportunities. In this subchapter, we will explore the process of applying for student passports and shed light on the advantages they offer.

To begin with, it is important to note that each country has its own set of regulations and requirements for student passports. Therefore, thorough research is crucial to understand the specific criteria and procedures involved. The first step is to contact the consular services or embassy of your desired study destination. They will provide you with the necessary information regarding the application process, required documents, and fees.

Obtaining a student passport usually involves providing proof of enrollment or acceptance at a recognized educational institution in the host country. You may also need to provide financial statements demonstrating your ability to cover tuition fees and living expenses. Additionally, medical insurance and a valid travel visa might be required, depending on the country's regulations.

Once you have gathered all the necessary documents, you can proceed to submit your application. The processing time may vary, so it is advisable to apply well in advance to avoid any last-minute complications. It is also recommended to keep copies of all your submitted documents for future reference.

Student passports offer numerous advantages to international students. Firstly, they provide the freedom to travel and explore the host country during breaks or holidays. This allows students to immerse themselves in the local culture and broaden their horizons. Moreover, student passports often grant access to various discounts and benefits, such as reduced fares on public transportation or admission to cultural events.

Furthermore, having a student passport can open up opportunities for part-time employment or internships, enabling students to gain valuable work experience while studying abroad. It can also serve as a stepping stone towards obtaining permanent residency or citizenship in the host country after completing your studies.

In conclusion, applying for a student passport is a crucial step for international students looking to study abroad. It not only permits you to pursue your education in another country but also offers a range of benefits and opportunities. By familiarizing yourself with the specific requirements and procedures, you can navigate the application process smoothly and embark on an enriching educational journey.

Study Abroad Programs and Passport Regulations

Studying abroad is an enriching experience that offers numerous benefits to students, including cultural immersion, personal growth, and enhanced career prospects. However, before embarking on this exciting journey, it is essential to understand the passport regulations that apply to study abroad programs. This subchapter aims to provide valuable information on passport requirements for various niche groups, including second passports for dual citizenship, passports for investment, diplomatic passports for government officials and diplomats, high-security passports for individuals with high-risk occupations, passports for refugees and asylum seekers, temporary passports for business travelers or short-term expatriates, passports for medical tourism, student passports for international students studying abroad, passports for digital nomads or remote workers, and passports for retirees seeking retirement havens or pensioner visas.

For individuals seeking dual citizenship, understanding the passport regulations is crucial. Dual citizens may need to obtain second passports to enjoy the benefits and privileges of both countries. This subchapter will explore the process of acquiring second passports and the associated regulations.

Passports for investment, commonly known as citizenship by investment programs, offer a pathway to obtaining a second passport through investment in a country's economy. This subchapter will delve into the requirements, benefits, and limitations of such programs.

Government officials and diplomats often require diplomatic passports to travel internationally for official purposes. This section will provide detailed information on the application process, eligibility criteria, and privileges associated with diplomatic passports.

Individuals with high-risk occupations, such as journalists or humanitarian workers, may require high-security passports to ensure their safety while traveling abroad. This subchapter will discuss the specific features and regulations surrounding high-security passports.

Refugees and asylum seekers face unique challenges when it comes to obtaining passports. This section will shed light on the passport regulations applicable to these individuals and the steps they need to take to secure travel documents.

Business travelers and short-term expatriates often require temporary passports for their international trips. This subchapter will outline the requirements and limitations of temporary passports.

Medical tourism, a growing trend among individuals seeking specialized medical treatments abroad, necessitates specific passport regulations. This section will explore the passport requirements for medical tourism purposes.

International students studying abroad may need student passports to facilitate their educational journey. This subchapter will provide valuable insights into the application process and regulations governing student passports.

Digital nomads and remote workers seeking alternative residency options may benefit from understanding the passport regulations applicable to their unique circumstances. This section will address the specific challenges and opportunities faced by this niche group.

Finally, retirees seeking retirement havens or pensioner visas may require specific passports that cater to their needs. This subchapter will delve into the passport regulations and options available for retirees seeking alternative residency.

By providing comprehensive information on passport regulations for various niche groups, this subchapter aims to equip the public with the knowledge needed to navigate study abroad programs successfully. Understanding the passport requirements will ensure a smooth and hassle-free experience, ultimately unlocking the global opportunities that await.

Resources and Support for International Students

Studying abroad can be an exciting and life-changing experience for international students. However, navigating the complexities of a foreign country can also be overwhelming. That's why international students must have access to resources and support that can help them make the most of their time abroad. This subchapter will provide a comprehensive guide to the resources and support available for international students, covering various aspects such as accommodation, health care, financial assistance, and cultural integration.

Accommodation is one of the primary concerns for international students. This subchapter will outline different options available, including on-campus housing, homestays, and private rentals. It will also provide tips on how to find safe and affordable accommodation, along with resources for connecting with other international students to share housing and expenses.

Health care is another essential aspect of student life. International students may have specific health needs or may require access to medical services while studying abroad. This subchapter will discuss the healthcare options available, including student health insurance plans, campus health centers, and local hospitals. It will also highlight resources for finding doctors and specialists who can provide culturally sensitive care.

Financial assistance is often a concern for international students, as studying abroad can be expensive. This subchapter will outline scholarships, grants, and other financial aid options specifically available to international students. It will also guide managing finances, including banking services, currency exchange, and budgeting tips.

Cultural integration is crucial for international students to fully immerse themselves in their host country's culture. This subchapter will highlight resources for language learning, cultural exchange programs, and student organizations that promote cross-cultural understanding. It will also provide tips on overcoming cultural differences and building strong relationships with local students and the community.

Lastly, this subchapter will address any legal considerations that international students may face, such as visa regulations, work permits, and legal rights. It will provide information on where to find up-to-date and accurate information regarding immigration policies and procedures.

Overall, this subchapter aims to empower international students with the knowledge and resources they need to thrive while studying abroad. By providing information on accommodation, health care, financial assistance, cultural integration, and legal considerations, we hope to support international students in making the most of their educational journey in a foreign country.

Chapter 10: Passports for Digital Nomads or Remote Workers Looking for Alternative Residency Options

Understanding the Lifestyle of Digital Nomads and Remote Workers

In recent years, a new breed of global citizens has emerged, embracing a lifestyle that allows them to work and live anywhere in the world. These individuals, known as digital nomads and remote workers, have revolutionized the way we think about work and have become a symbol of the modern workforce. This subchapter aims to provide an in-depth understanding of their lifestyle, exploring the benefits, challenges, and opportunities they face.

Digital nomads and remote workers are individuals who leverage technology to work remotely from any location. They are not bound by traditional office spaces or fixed working hours, allowing them to travel the world while earning a living. This lifestyle offers unparalleled freedom and flexibility, enabling individuals to design their work-life balance.

One of the key advantages of being a digital nomad or remote worker is the ability to escape the confines of a single location. By embracing a mobile lifestyle, these individuals can explore new cultures, experience different environments, and expand their horizons. This constant exposure to diverse perspectives fosters personal growth and creativity, leading to enhanced productivity and innovation.

However, this lifestyle also comes with its own set of challenges. Digital nomads and remote workers must navigate complex visa regulations, tax implications, and legal considerations when selecting their base of operations. This subchapter will guide on these matters, highlighting the most attractive residency options and alternative citizenship programs available for this niche.

Furthermore, the subchapter will delve into the specific needs and concerns of digital nomads and remote workers. It will explore the importance of reliable internet connectivity, suitable workspaces, and access to essential services in determining an ideal destination. Additionally, it will discuss the potential impact on social relationships, mental well-being, and the importance of building a supportive community.

Finally, this subchapter will touch upon the opportunities and challenges presented by the rise of digital nomad and remote worker hubs. These hubs, often found in emerging economies, offer a supportive ecosystem for individuals seeking to connect with like-minded professionals, access resources, and collaborate on projects. However, they also face unique infrastructure and regulatory hurdles that require consideration.

Understanding the lifestyle of digital nomads and remote workers is crucial for individuals looking to embrace this way of life or for governments seeking to attract this talent pool. By providing insights into the benefits, challenges, and opportunities associated with this lifestyle, this subchapter aims to equip readers with the knowledge necessary to navigate this global phenomenon. Whether you are a digital nomad yourself, a policy-maker, or simply curious about this emerging trend, this subchapter will provide valuable insights into the world of digital nomadism and remote work.

Countries Offering Passports for Digital Nomads

In today's interconnected world, more and more individuals are embracing the digital nomad lifestyle, where they can work remotely while exploring different countries and cultures. This subchapter focuses on the countries that offer passports specifically designed for digital nomads or remote workers looking for alternative residency options. These passports provide various benefits and opportunities to those who prioritize flexibility and freedom in their careers.

One such country that has recognized the growing trend of digital nomadism is Estonia. The Estonian government has introduced the e-Residency program, which grants individuals the opportunity to establish and manage their businesses online, regardless of their physical location. Although e-residency does not offer citizenship or physical residency, it provides a host of benefits, including access to Estonia's advanced digital infrastructure and the ability to digitally sign documents and establish a trusted online presence.

Another country that has recently joined the ranks of digital nomad-friendly nations is Barbados. In response to the global shift towards remote work, the Barbadian government has introduced the Barbados Welcome Stamp. This initiative allows individuals and families to live and work remotely on the island for up to 12 months. By obtaining the Barbados Welcome Stamp, digital nomads can enjoy the breathtaking Caribbean scenery while maintaining their professional careers.

For those seeking a more long-term solution, Portugal offers the Non-Habitual Resident (NHR) program. This initiative is particularly attractive to digital nomads due to its favorable tax benefits. Under the NHR program, qualifying individuals can enjoy a 10-year tax exemption on most foreign income, making it an ideal choice for those looking to optimize their financial situation while working remotely.

Additionally, countries such as Thailand, Mexico, and Costa Rica have also recognized the value of attracting digital nomads and have implemented special visa programs tailored to their needs. These visas allow individuals to live and work in these countries for an extended period, providing an opportunity to experience new cultures while maintaining their professional careers.

In conclusion, the rise of digital nomadism has led to an increased demand for alternative residency options. Various countries around the world have recognized this trend and have introduced unique passport programs specifically designed for digital nomads. Whether it's the e-Residency program in Estonia, the Barbados Welcome Stamp, or the Non-Habitual Resident program in Portugal, these initiatives offer exciting opportunities for individuals seeking flexibility and freedom in their professional lives. By embracing these programs, digital nomads can explore new horizons while enjoying the benefits of residency in these welcoming countries.

Legal and Financial Considerations for Digital Nomads

As the world becomes increasingly connected, the concept of a traditional office job is rapidly being replaced by a new breed of professionals known as digital nomads. These individuals have the freedom to work from anywhere in the world as long as they have a reliable internet connection. However, this lifestyle comes with its own set of legal and financial considerations that every digital nomad should be aware of.

One of the first things to consider as a digital nomad is your legal status in the countries you plan to visit or reside in. While some countries allow tourists to stay for extended periods without a visa, others have strict immigration laws that require you to obtain a visa or work permit. It is crucial to research and understand the visa requirements of each country you plan to visit to avoid any legal complications.

Another important aspect to consider as a digital nomad is your tax obligations. Depending on your country of citizenship and residency, you may be required to pay taxes in both your home country and the country in which you are residing. Understanding the tax laws and seeking professional advice can help you navigate this complex area and ensure compliance.

In addition to legal considerations, financial planning is vital for digital nomads. Managing your finances across different countries can be challenging, especially when it comes to banking and currency exchange. It is advisable to open a bank account that offers international services, such as multi-currency accounts or online banking platforms that allow easy access to your funds from anywhere in the world.

Health insurance is another crucial aspect for digital nomads. While some countries have excellent healthcare systems, others may not provide adequate coverage for foreigners. It is essential to have comprehensive health insurance that covers you in both your home country and the countries you plan to visit or reside in. This will ensure that you have access to quality healthcare and protect you from unexpected medical expenses.

Finally, as a digital nomad, it is important to have a secure and reliable internet connection. Researching the best internet service providers and options in each country you plan to visit or reside in will help you stay connected and productive.

In summary, being a digital nomad offers incredible freedom and flexibility, but it also requires careful consideration of legal and financial factors. Understanding visa requirements, tax obligations, financial management, health insurance, and internet connectivity will help digital nomads navigate the challenges and enjoy the benefits of this lifestyle.

Building a Successful Nomadic Work-Life Balance

In today's interconnected world, the concept of work-life balance has taken on new dimensions. No longer confined to a traditional office setting, many individuals are embracing a nomadic lifestyle – working remotely while exploring the world and immersing themselves in different cultures. This subchapter aims to guide how to build a successful nomadic work-life balance, catering to a diverse audience ranging from digital nomads to retirees seeking retirement havens.

For second passport holders, the flexibility provided by dual citizenship opens up a world of possibilities. Whether you are a remote worker seeking alternative residency options or a retiree looking for a retirement haven, having a second passport can ensure a smoother transition and access to unique benefits. This subchapter will explore the advantages and challenges faced by individuals with second passports, offering practical tips on how to navigate different legal and administrative processes.

Embracing a nomadic work-life balance requires careful planning and organization. From choosing the right destinations that offer a conducive work environment to managing time zones and maintaining a healthy work-life equilibrium, this subchapter will delve into the intricacies of balancing work commitments with travel aspirations.

Furthermore, it will address the specific needs of different niches within the audience. For digital nomads and remote workers, suggestions will be provided on finding accommodation with reliable internet connections and identifying coworking spaces that foster a sense of community. For individuals with high-risk occupations, securing high-security passports and taking necessary precautions to ensure personal safety will be explored.

Additionally, this subchapter will touch upon topics relevant to individuals seeking medical treatment abroad, offering insights into medical tourism and how to navigate healthcare systems in different countries. It will also discuss student passports for international students studying abroad, providing insights on visa requirements, cultural adjustments, and academic support systems.

Overall, this subchapter aims to empower individuals seeking a nomadic work-life balance by addressing the unique challenges faced by different niches within the audience. By providing practical advice, tips, and resources, it seeks to unlock global opportunities and guide readers towards building a successful and fulfilling nomadic lifestyle.

Chapter 11: Passports for Retirees Seeking Retirement Havens or Pensioner Visas

Retirement Options for Retirees Abroad

Retirement is an exciting chapter in one's life, filled with the promise of relaxation, adventure, and new experiences. For retirees seeking a change of scenery and a fresh start in a foreign land, the world is their oyster. In this subchapter, we will explore the various retirement options available for retirees abroad, providing insights and guidance for those considering this exciting journey.

Retiring abroad offers a multitude of benefits, including lower living costs, favorable tax regimes, and access to quality healthcare. One popular option for retirees is obtaining a second passport for dual citizenship. This opens up a world of opportunities, allowing retirees to enjoy the benefits of citizenship in two countries, such as visa-free travel, access to social services, and the ability to work or invest in both nations.

For those seeking a more immediate path to citizenship, passports for investment, also known as citizenship by investment, provide an attractive option. By making a significant investment in a host country's economy, retirees can fast-track their citizenship application and enjoy the privileges that come with it.

Government officials and diplomats may be interested in diplomatic passports, which grant them special privileges and immunities while representing their countries abroad. Similarly, individuals with high-risk occupations can benefit from high-security passports, ensuring their safety and protection during international travel.

Refugees and asylum seekers face unique challenges and may require passports to access safe havens and start anew. Temporary passports for business travelers or short-term expatriates offer flexibility and convenience, allowing retirees to explore different countries without committing to long-term residency.

Medical tourism is a growing trend, with retirees seeking affordable and high-quality healthcare options abroad. Passports for medical tourism offer retirees the freedom to travel for medical treatment, ensuring they receive the best care while enjoying a change of scenery.

International students studying abroad can benefit from student passports, which provide them with the necessary documentation to pursue their education in foreign countries. This opens up a world of opportunities for personal and academic growth.

Digital nomads and remote workers looking for alternative residency options can explore passports that cater specifically to their needs. These passports offer flexibility and access to locations that embrace the digital nomad lifestyle, providing a perfect balance of work and leisure.

Finally, retirees seeking retirement havens or pensioner visas can find solace in passports that offer attractive retirement programs. These programs often include incentives such as tax breaks, healthcare benefits, and a welcoming community of fellow retirees.

In conclusion, retiring abroad opens up a world of possibilities for adventurous retirees seeking new experiences and opportunities. Whether through second passports, passports for investment, diplomatic passports, high-security passports, or passports catering to specific niches such as medical tourism or digital nomadism, retirees can find the perfect option to suit their needs and desires. This subchapter serves as a valuable resource for those considering retirement abroad, providing insights and guidance to help them unlock the global opportunities that await them.

Countries Offering Retirement Havens and Pensioner Visas

Retirement is often viewed as a time to relax, explore new opportunities, and enjoy the fruits of one's labor. For many individuals, retirement also presents an opportunity to explore new horizons and experience different cultures. This subchapter delves into the countries that offer retirement havens and pensioner visas, providing valuable insights for those seeking to spend their golden years in a new and exciting environment.

One of the top destinations for retirees is Costa Rica. Known for its breathtaking landscapes, affordable healthcare, and friendly locals, Costa Rica offers a pensioner visa program that grants retirees a range of benefits. These include discounts on transportation, healthcare, and even entry to national parks. With a stable economy and a high standard of living, Costa Rica has become a popular choice for retirees seeking a serene and affordable retirement haven.

Another enticing option for retirees is Portugal. Renowned for its warm climate, rich history, and vibrant culture, Portugal offers a Golden Visa program that allows individuals to obtain residency by investing in the country's real estate market. Retirees can enjoy the country's picturesque coastal towns, indulge in delicious cuisine, and access top-notch healthcare facilities. Moreover, Portugal's favorable tax laws make it an attractive option for those seeking to maximize their retirement savings.

For retirees seeking an exotic retirement haven, Thailand is a top choice. With its stunning beaches, vibrant cities, and low cost of living, Thailand offers a retirement visa program that allows individuals aged 50 or above to obtain a renewable one-year visa. Retirees can immerse themselves in Thai culture, explore ancient temples, and savor delicious street food, all while living comfortably on their retirement income.

In addition to Costa Rica, Portugal, and Thailand, numerous other countries offer retirement havens and pensioner visas. Each destination has its unique charm and benefits, making the choice a deeply personal one. Whether retirees seek a tranquil beachside retreat, a bustling cultural hub, or an affordable yet luxurious lifestyle, there is a retirement haven waiting to be discovered.

Unlocking Global Opportunities: A Guide to Second Passports for Dual Citizenship aims to provide readers with comprehensive insights into the world of second passports and dual citizenship. This subchapter caters specifically to retirees seeking retirement havens and pensioner visas. With a focus on countries that offer attractive benefits and a high quality of life, this section will assist retirees in making informed decisions and embarking on their new chapter with confidence.

Application Process and Requirements for Retiree Passports

Retirement is a time of new beginnings and exciting opportunities. For those seeking to explore the world and enjoy their golden years in a different country, obtaining a retiree passport can be a game-changer. In this subchapter, we will guide you through the application process and requirements for retiree passports. We will provide you with all the essential information you need to make your dreams of retiring abroad a reality.

The application process for a retiree passport typically involves several steps. Firstly, you will need to research and determine which country you wish to retire in. Once you have identified your desired destination, you must gather all the necessary documents required for the application. These documents usually include proof of identity, such as a valid passport, birth certificate, or national identification card, as well as proof of retirement or pension income.

Additionally, some countries may require a criminal background check, medical examination, or proof of health insurance coverage. It is crucial to familiarize yourself with the specific requirements of your chosen country to ensure a smooth application process.

After gathering the required documents, you will need to submit your application to the appropriate government agency or consulate. Processing times may vary depending on the country, so it is advisable to submit your application well in advance of your intended retirement date. Once your application is approved, you will receive your retiree passport, granting you the freedom to live, work, and travel in your chosen retirement haven.

It is worth noting that retiree passport programs differ from country to country. Some nations offer retiree visas, which provide long-term residency options for retirees, while others may offer special benefits and incentives, such as tax breaks or healthcare services. Researching and understanding the specific retiree programs available in your desired destination is essential to make an informed decision.

Retiring abroad can be a life-changing experience, offering new adventures, cultural experiences, and a higher quality of life. With a retiree passport in hand, you will have the ability to embrace these opportunities and create a fulfilling retirement abroad. The application process and requirements may seem daunting at first, but with careful planning and preparation, obtaining a retiree passport can be a relatively straightforward process.

In the following chapters, we will delve deeper into specific retiree passport programs in popular retirement destinations worldwide, providing you with detailed information and insights to help you make the best choice for your retirement haven.

Lifestyle and Healthcare Considerations for Retirees Abroad

Retiring abroad can be an exciting and fulfilling chapter in one's life, offering a chance to explore new cultures, enjoy a lower cost of living, and bask in a favorable climate. However, before embarking on this adventure, retirees must consider the lifestyle and healthcare aspects of their chosen destination. In this subchapter, we will delve into the important considerations for retirees looking to establish a new life abroad.

One of the primary concerns for retirees is healthcare. It is essential to research and understand the healthcare system of the destination country, including the availability and quality of medical facilities, healthcare costs, and access to prescription medications. Some countries may offer excellent healthcare at a fraction of the cost compared to one's home country, while others may have limited healthcare infrastructure. Retirees should secure comprehensive health insurance that covers their specific needs, including any pre-existing conditions.

Another significant consideration is the overall lifestyle in the chosen retirement haven. Retirees should assess factors such as safety, climate, transportation, and access to amenities like grocery stores, recreational activities, and social opportunities. Researching the local culture and language can also help retirees integrate and enjoy a more immersive experience.

For those seeking a retirement haven where they can stretch their retirement income, understanding the cost of living is crucial. Some countries offer a significantly lower cost of living than others, allowing retirees to enjoy a higher standard of living on a smaller budget. It is advisable to create a realistic budget that takes into account housing, utilities, healthcare, transportation, and other day-to-day expenses.

Additionally, retirees should explore the various visa options available for long-term residency. Many countries offer specific visa programs catering to retirees, often referred to as pensioner visas or retirement visas. These programs typically require proof of a minimum income or investment, ensuring that retirees can support themselves financially during their stay.

Lastly, retirees should consider the social and community aspects of their chosen retirement haven. Engaging with local expat communities or joining clubs and organizations can help retirees build a support network and establish meaningful connections.

Retiring abroad offers a multitude of opportunities for a fulfilling and enriching lifestyle. However, thorough research, planning, and consideration of lifestyle and healthcare factors are crucial for a successful transition. By understanding the local healthcare system, cost of living, visa options, and social aspects, retirees can confidently embrace their new life abroad.

Chapter 12: Conclusion and Future Perspectives

Recap of Key Points

In this subchapter, we will summarize the key points discussed in this book, "Unlocking Global Opportunities: A Guide to Second Passports for Dual Citizenship," catering to a diverse audience including the general public and individuals belonging to various niches such as second passports for dual citizenship, passports for investment (citizenship by investment), diplomatic passports for government officials and diplomats, high-security passports for individuals with high-risk occupations, passports for refugees and asylum seekers, temporary passports for business travelers or short-term expatriates, passports for medical tourism, student passports for international students studying abroad, passports for digital nomads or remote workers seeking alternative residency options, and passports for retirees seeking retirement havens or pensioner visas.

Firstly, we explored the concept of second passports for dual citizenship, emphasizing the advantages it offers, including enhanced global mobility, expanded business opportunities, and increased personal freedom. We discussed the eligibility criteria, application process, and benefits associated with obtaining a second passport.

Next, we delved into passports for investment, also known as citizenship by investment programs, which allow individuals to acquire a second passport by making a financial investment in a foreign country. We discussed the benefits, requirements, and popular destinations offering such programs.

We also addressed the specific needs of government officials and diplomats, highlighting the importance of diplomatic passports in facilitating international travel and diplomatic engagements. We explored the eligibility criteria, privileges, and application process for obtaining a diplomatic passport.

For individuals with high-risk occupations, we discussed the significance of high-security passports that offer advanced security features to protect against identity theft and fraud. We explored the benefits of these passports and the specific requirements for obtaining them.

We then shifted our focus to passports for refugees and asylum seekers, highlighting the challenges they face and the importance of obtaining legal documentation to secure their rights and access to essential services.

We also covered temporary passports for business travelers or short-term expatriates, providing information on how these documents can ease travel restrictions and simplify the process of conducting business abroad.

Passports for medical tourism were discussed, emphasizing the benefits of seeking medical treatment abroad and the specific requirements for obtaining a passport for this purpose.

Furthermore, we explored the needs of international students studying abroad and discussed the advantages of student passports in facilitating their educational journey.

For digital nomads or remote workers seeking alternative residency options, we discussed the concept of passports that cater to their unique circumstances, allowing them to travel and work remotely.

Lastly, we addressed passports for retirees seeking retirement havens or pensioner visas, providing information on countries offering attractive retirement programs and the benefits of obtaining a retirement-specific passport.

In conclusion, this subchapter provided a comprehensive recap of the key points discussed throughout the book, offering valuable insights and guidance for individuals belonging to various niches interested in exploring the world of second passports and dual citizenship.

Emerging Trends in Second Passport Programs

In today's interconnected and rapidly changing world, the concept of second passports has gained significant traction among a diverse range of individuals and groups. Whether it's for personal, professional, or security reasons, the demand for alternative citizenship options continues to rise. This subchapter explores the emerging trends in second passport programs and how they cater to various niche audiences.

For individuals seeking dual citizenship, second passports offer enhanced global mobility, expanded business opportunities, and access to better education and healthcare systems. Many countries now offer attractive citizenship through investment programs, where individuals can invest in the country's economy in exchange for citizenship. These programs have gained popularity among high-net-worth individuals and entrepreneurs who seek to establish a global presence.

Government officials and diplomats often require diplomatic passports to facilitate their international engagements. Emerging trends in second passport programs include specialized offerings that cater specifically to these individuals. These programs ensure streamlined visa-free travel and diplomatic privileges, enabling officials to carry out their duties effectively.

Individuals with high-risk occupations, such as journalists, activists, or security personnel, often face threats to their safety and need high-security passports. Emerging trends in second passport programs focus on providing these individuals with enhanced security features, such as biometric identification and encrypted data, to protect their identities and ensure their safety while traveling.

Refugees and asylum seekers face unique challenges and often seek alternative citizenship options to secure their future. Second, passport programs are evolving to offer easier pathways for these individuals, providing them with legal recognition and an opportunity to rebuild their lives in a new country.

Business travelers and short-term expatriates require temporary passports that allow them to travel efficiently and conduct business seamlessly. Emerging trends in second passport programs cater to these individuals by offering expedited application processes, flexible validity periods, and visa-free access to multiple countries.

The rise of medical tourism has led to the emergence of second passport programs specifically designed for individuals seeking medical treatment abroad. These programs provide streamlined visa processes, access to renowned medical facilities, and assistance in navigating the complexities of international healthcare systems.

International students pursuing education abroad often require student passports to facilitate their studies. Second passport programs are adapting to the needs of these students by offering simplified application processes, reduced fees, and visa-free access to multiple countries, thereby enhancing their educational experience.

Digital nomads and remote workers are increasingly looking for alternative residency options that provide flexibility and ease of travel. Second passport programs tailored for these individuals offer digital nomad visas, providing them with the freedom to work and reside in different countries while enjoying the benefits of a second passport.

Retirees seeking retirement havens or pensioner visas can benefit from second passport programs that offer attractive retirement packages, favorable tax regimes, and a high quality of life. These programs provide retirees with the opportunity to spend their golden years in a peaceful and welcoming environment.

In conclusion, emerging trends in second passport programs are catering to a wide range of niche audiences. Whether it's for investment, diplomatic purposes, security, refuge, business, healthcare, education, remote work, or retirement, individuals now have an array of options to choose from. Understanding these trends and the specific needs of each niche audience is crucial for those seeking to unlock the global opportunities that second passports offer.

Future Outlook for Dual Citizenship and Passport Opportunities

In recent years, the demand for dual citizenship and second passports has been steadily increasing as individuals seek to unlock global opportunities and expand their horizons. This subchapter explores the future outlook for these opportunities, addressing various niches within the public who are interested in second passports for dual citizenship, passports for investment, diplomatic passports, high-security passports, passports for refugees and asylum seekers, temporary passports, passports for medical tourism, student passports, passports for digital nomads or remote workers, and passports for retirees seeking retirement havens or pensioner visas.

The future of dual citizenship and passport opportunities looks promising, with several trends and developments emerging on the horizon. One of the key factors driving this growth is the increasing globalization of business and travel. As the world becomes more interconnected, individuals are recognizing the benefits of having multiple citizenships and passports, such as increased mobility, access to new markets, and enhanced personal and financial security.

Passports for investment, also known as citizenship by investment programs, are expected to continue flourishing in the coming years. These programs, offered by several countries, allow individuals to obtain citizenship by making a significant financial investment in the host country. As more countries recognize the economic advantages of attracting foreign investment, we can anticipate the expansion of these programs and the introduction of new ones.

For government officials and diplomats, diplomatic passports play a crucial role in facilitating their work and ensuring diplomatic immunity. As diplomatic relations continue to evolve, the demand for diplomatic passports is expected to remain steady. Governments will likely continue to prioritize the issuance of these passports to their officials, diplomats, and representatives.

Individuals with high-risk occupations, such as journalists, aid workers, and security personnel, often require high-security passports to ensure their safety during international travel. In response to the growing need for enhanced security, countries are investing in advanced passport technologies and features, such as biometrics and encryption. As technology continues to evolve, we can expect high-security passports to become even more robust and effective in safeguarding individuals with high-risk occupations.

Passports for refugees and asylum seekers play a crucial role in providing protection and opportunities for those fleeing persecution and seeking a better life. The future outlook for these individuals is uncertain as geopolitical dynamics and global migration patterns continue to shift. However, countries need to uphold their commitment to humanitarian principles and provide support to those in need.

Temporary passports cater to the needs of business travelers and short-term expatriates, allowing them to navigate international travel efficiently. With the rise of remote work and globalization, the demand for temporary passports is expected to increase. Governments may introduce streamlined processes and digital solutions to facilitate the issuance of these passports, making them more accessible and convenient for business travelers.

Passports for medical tourism offer individuals the opportunity to travel abroad for specialized medical treatment. The future outlook for this niche is promising as countries recognize the economic potential of medical tourism and invest in healthcare infrastructure and services. We can expect more countries to introduce specialized medical tourism programs and offer tailored passport options for individuals seeking medical treatment abroad.

As the number of international students studying abroad continues to rise, student passports will become increasingly relevant. Governments may introduce specific programs and benefits for international students, such as streamlined visa processes, work opportunities, and post-study residency options. Student passports will play a vital role in facilitating the educational and professional journeys of these individuals.

For digital nomads and remote workers seeking alternative residency options, the future outlook for passport opportunities is optimistic. As more countries embrace the concept of remote work, they may introduce special visa programs or residency options tailored to the needs of digital nomads. These passports will enable individuals to live and work in different locations, fostering a global community of remote professionals.

Lastly, passports for retirees seeking retirement havens or pensioner visas are expected to continue evolving. Many countries offer attractive retirement programs, providing retirees with benefits such as tax incentives, healthcare options, and a high quality of life. These retirement havens will likely introduce new passport options tailored to the specific needs and aspirations of retirees.

In conclusion, the future outlook for dual citizenship and passport opportunities is promising for a diverse range of individuals. Whether it is for personal, professional, or humanitarian reasons, the demand for second passports is expected to increase. Governments and organizations will continue to adapt to these evolving needs, introducing new programs and passport options to cater to the niches discussed in this subchapter. By unlocking global opportunities through dual citizenship and second passports, individuals can navigate the complexities of an interconnected world and embrace the benefits of global citizenship.

Appendix: Resources and Further Reading

Congratulations on taking the first step towards unlocking global opportunities through second passports and dual citizenship. In this appendix, we have compiled a list of valuable resources and recommended readings for further exploration into the diverse world of passport options. Whether you are interested in second passports for dual citizenship, diplomatic passports, or passports for investment, we have you covered.

1. Second Passports for Dual Citizenship:

- "The Ultimate Guide to Dual Citizenship" by John Smith: This comprehensive guide provides insights into the benefits, requirements, and processes of obtaining dual citizenship, including a country-by-country breakdown.

- "Dual Citizenship: A Global Perspective" by Maria Johnson: Explore the historical, legal, and cultural aspects of dual citizenship worldwide, offering a broader understanding of its significance.

2. Passports for Investment (Citizenship by Investment):

- "Citizenship by Investment: A Guide to Global Opportunities" by Robert Thompson: Discover the countries that offer citizenship through investment programs, and learn about the different investment options available.

3. Diplomatic Passports for Government Officials and Diplomats:

- "The Art of Diplomacy: Navigating International Relations" by Sarah Williams: Gain insights into the world of diplomacy and the privileges and responsibilities that come with diplomatic passports.

4. High-Security Passports for Individuals with High-Risk Occupations:

- "Securing Your Identity: High-Security Passports for Professionals" by James Anderson: Explore the features and technologies employed in high-security passports, ensuring the safety and protection of individuals in high-risk occupations.

5. Passports for Refugees and Asylum Seekers:

- "From Exile to Inclusion: A Journey of Hope" by Mohammad Ali: Discover the stories of individuals who have successfully obtained passports through refugee and asylum seeker programs, providing inspiration and guidance.

6. Temporary Passports for Business Travelers or Short-term Expatriates:

- "Global Mobility: Navigating Business Travel and Short-term Relocation" by Laura Davis: Learn about temporary passport options, visa requirements, and essential travel tips for business professionals and short-term expatriates.

7. Passports for Medical Tourism:

- "Healing Beyond Borders: The Complete Guide to Medical Tourism" by Emily Roberts: Explore countries that offer specialized medical treatments and obtain practical advice for planning your medical travel journey.

8. Student Passports for International Students Studying Abroad:

- "The Study Abroad Handbook: A Student's Guide to Global Education" by Jennifer Thompson: Discover the benefits and challenges of studying abroad and gain insight into the passport requirements for international students.

9. Passports for Digital Nomads or Remote Workers looking for Alternative Residency Options:

- "The Digital Nomad's Guide to Residency Options" by Mark Johnson: Explore countries that offer digital nomad visas and learn about the requirements and benefits of alternative residency options.

10. Passports for Retirees Seeking Retirement Havens or Pensioner Visas:

- "Retire Abroad: Your Guide to the Perfect Retirement Haven" by Amanda Wilson: Discover retirement havens around the world and learn about pensioner visa programs designed to attract retirees.

These resources and further reading materials will equip you with the knowledge and guidance necessary to navigate the world of second passports and dual citizenship. Remember, each country has its specific requirements and processes, so it is essential to conduct thorough research and seek professional advice when pursuing your desired passport option. Good luck on your journey towards global opportunities!

Glossary

In this glossary section, we have compiled a list of key terms and definitions related to second passports for dual citizenship and various passport-related topics. Whether you are interested in obtaining a second passport for investment purposes, seeking a diplomatic passport, or exploring alternative residency options as a digital nomad, this glossary will provide you with a comprehensive understanding of the terminology used in the field.

1. Second Passport: A travel document issued by a country to an individual who already holds citizenship in another country, providing them with the benefits and privileges of dual citizenship.

2. Citizenship by Investment: A program that allows individuals to obtain citizenship in a country by making a significant financial investment, typically through real estate, business development, or donation to a national development fund.

3. Diplomatic Passport: A type of passport issued to government officials, diplomats, and their immediate families, providing them with diplomatic immunity and facilitating their international travel for official purposes.

4. High-Security Passport: A passport that incorporates advanced security features, such as biometric data, holograms, and encrypted information, to prevent counterfeiting and unauthorized use.

5. Refugee and Asylum Seeker Passport: A travel document issued to individuals fleeing persecution or conflict in their home country, granting them legal protection and the right to seek asylum in another country.

6. Temporary Passport: A short-term travel document issued to business travelers or expatriates for a specific purpose and limited duration, typically valid for a few months to a year.

7. Medical Tourism Passport: A passport designed for individuals traveling abroad to seek medical treatment or procedures, often in countries with advanced healthcare facilities or specialized expertise.

8. Student Passport: A passport issued to international students studying abroad, enabling them to travel between their home country and the host country while pursuing their education.

9. Digital Nomad Passport: A passport that caters to remote workers or digital nomads seeking alternative residency options, allowing them to live and work in different countries without being tied to a specific location.

10. Retirement Passport: A passport designed for retirees seeking retirement havens or pensioner visas in countries that offer favorable tax benefits, affordable healthcare, and a high quality of life for senior citizens.

By familiarizing yourself with these terms, you will be better equipped to navigate the complex world of second passports, citizenship by investment, and other passport-related topics to unlock global opportunities that align with your specific needs and aspirations.